Praying Through

Hidden Truths to Receiving Answered Prayer

Sara Steele with Susan Janos

DESTINY IMAGE® PUBLISHERS, INC.
P.O. Box 310, Shippensburg, PA 17257-0310
"Speaking to the Purposes of God for This Generation and for the Generations to Come."

This book and all other Destiny Image, Revival Press, MercyPlace, Fresh Bread, Destiny Image Fiction, and Treasure House books are available at Christian bookstores and distributors worldwide.

For a U.S. bookstore nearest you, call 1-800-722-6774.
For more information on foreign distributors, call 717-532-3040.
Reach us on the Internet: www.destinyimage.com.

ISBN 13 Trade Paper: 978-0-7684-3648-8
ISBN 13 Hard Copy: 978-0-7684-3649-5
ISBN 13 Large Print: 978-0-7684-3650-1
ISBN 13 E-book: 978-0-7684-9038-1

For Worldwide Distribution, Printed in the U.S.A.
1 2 3 4 5 6 7 8 9 10 / 14 13 12 11

Endorsements

I have known Sara Steele since 1980. Her sister was a member of my church when I was a pastor in Yankton, South Dakota. Thus, I became friends with the family, and we have remained friends over the years. I have wonderful memories of our times of fellowship and prayer.

Sara has lived a life of prayer. When I need some prayer support, I know who to call. This book will be a great blessing to your life as you begin your journey of *praying through*.

—Reverend Gary DeVoe
Media Director,
Faith Christian Fellowship International
Tulsa, Oklahoma

Sara Steele has made the subject of *praying through* very practical, understandable, and exciting.

When you finish reading this book, the first thing you will want to do is pray!

—Paul Crouch
President and Founder,
Trinity Broadcasting Network
Santa Ana, California

There are those who don't want their prayers to change anything, least of all themselves. But if you're ready to see God bare His arm on your behalf and on behalf of all for whom you pray, you've picked up the right book. Sara Steele's *Praying Through* will teach you how to allow God to use your prayer life to accomplish all that He wants to accomplish both in you and in your world.

—Harald Bredesen
Minister, Author, and CBN Founding
Board Member
Escondido, California

Contents

Foreword

As a young man, I asked, "Why pray?" The Bible says God knows our needs before we ask and He certainly doesn't need our advice. The simple answer—and all we really need to know—is we pray because He tells us to.

That answer is enough, but leaves us even more intrigued. "Why does He tell us to pray?"

One of many reasons we should pray is God wants us in *the loop*, part of the process, in the inner circle. He doesn't need us to tell Him anything, but He enjoys spending time with us, communicating with us, planning and working with us. And He knows time in His presence strengthens us, builds character, enhances wisdom, gives us faith, and makes us faithful. The more we're with Him, the more we grow to be like Him.

In other words, prayer is far more than presenting a to-do list to God. That's why He doesn't just want us to pray, but to *pray through*.

Some of us believe when Paul told Timothy, *"...in the last days perilous times shall come"* (2 Tim. 3:1), he spoke of our day. If so, surely it is time to go beyond perfunctory prayer and learn to touch the heart of God. There are those who don't want their prayers to change anything, least of all themselves. But if you're ready to see God bare His arm on your behalf and on behalf of all for whom you pray, you've picked up the right book. Sara Steele's *Praying Through* will teach you how to allow God to use your prayer life to accomplish all He wants to accomplish both in you and in your world.

—Harald Bredesen
Minister, Author, and Founding Board Member
Christian Broadcasting Network

Introduction

"How long should you pray each day?" I asked my mother-in-law. She and my father-in-law had just come to pastor the church where my husband and I lived.

She replied, "Just pray until you *pray through.*"

She knew the secret to receiving remarkable answers to prayer—a secret that would change my life and the lives of my family forever.

Many believers in the early to mid 1900s knew the power of *praying through* and experienced amazing healings and miracles, but this vital truth has been almost completely lost today. What I'm about to share with you has saved the lives of my children, healed my body, brought miraculous intervention in a host of challenges, and helped thousands of people. After 50 years of *praying through*, I'll share with you in the following pages what I *know* works.

Chapter 1

Holy Spirit-Led Prayers

On a cool spring evening in our five-bedroom farmhouse, I was visiting and praying with my sister Mary Ruth and my friend Gwendolyn. Gwendolyn felt strongly that we needed to pray for my youngest daughter. She had driven to Minneapolis with several friends.

As we began to pray, a great burden for her safety came to my sister and me. We prayed for just a short time, but both Mary Ruth and I continued to feel burdened in our spirits. Gwendolyn kept saying, "You only have to pray once." The burden still did not lift. My sister and I prayed for 45 minutes longer until we finally felt a release—the burden lifted. We had *prayed through*. Once we felt that release in our spirits, we stopped praying.

My daughter shared with us later that her life was in grave danger that day. She had gone to a concert in a large venue with her friends. Somehow she became separated from them and started to feel ill. She blacked out in the middle of thousands of people. When she woke up, someone was carrying her to an open space in the concert hall. The person asked if she was going to be OK and then disappeared. She was not hurt or robbed and was able to find her friends and get help. We know prayer saved her life that day.

The Secret

The secret to *praying through* is really this: pray until the burden you feel in your spirit lifts or pray until you feel a release that the work is done. You might receive the answer right away or it might come later, but you have a peace and a knowing inside that the spiritual battle is won.

Praying through the situations of life brings powerful answers from the Spirit of God and causes your confidence in prayer to soar. With God, nothing really is impossible. The challenge is recognizing when you receive a burden and doing what it takes to pray through it. That is what you will discover in the following pages.

The Holy Spirit Knows

Only the Holy Spirit knew the danger my daughter was in and what prayer needed to be prayed. I had to listen to the Holy Spirit's guidance and act on the way He led me to pray. Even though I didn't know exactly what was wrong, it was important for me to contend until I prayed through. The apostle John instructs us:

Howbeit when He, the Spirit of truth, is come, He will guide you into all truth: for He shall not speak of Himself; but whatsoever He shall hear, that shall He speak: and He will shew you things to come (John 16:13).

We see from this Scripture the Holy Spirit has been sent to help us and to guide us into truth. It is so important to pray with the help of the Holy Spirit. Without Him we are limited by our natural minds, but with Him we enter into a supernatural realm where we can pray accurately and effectively.

In First Samuel 1:12, Hannah *prayed through* to bear a child. In First Kings 18, the prophet Elijah prayed for rain on Mount Carmel, but it took seven times until the rain cloud appeared. In the New Testament, Jesus Christ often took time to pray alone and later performed many miracles. In Acts 12, the church prayed until an angel helped Peter escape from prison. With the direction of the Holy Spirit, we can *pray through* in the same way as we see in the Scriptures.

The Holy Spirit Is Our Helper

The Holy Spirit is the Spirit of God. Jesus sent Him to be our Helper here on the earth. The Father God, Jesus Christ the Son, and Holy Spirit are all God. They are three in one. Sometimes they are called the God-head, which means they are all God.

I like to use the example of an egg to explain the God-head, also referred to as the Trinity. An egg has three parts—the shell, the yolk, and the white—but it is still one egg. God is the same way. God the Father, Jesus the Son, and the Holy Spirit are all God. In the Book of John we find that the Holy Spirit was sent by Jesus to be our Comforter, Teacher, and Helper (see John 14:26). When we are born again into the Kingdom of God, God comes in us and we also live in God. The apostle Paul stated it like this, *"In Him we live and move and have our being..."* (Acts 17:28). Jesus dwells in us and we are in Him, the way He is in the heavenly Father and the Father is in Him. The facilitator for this relationship is the Holy Spirit, the third part of the Trinity, and He is here now to help us pray through.

The Scriptures Are Our Guide

The Lord has also left us His Word, the Bible, as our guidebook. Whatever we do must agree with what the Bible teaches. The Holy Spirit will never lead you to do anything unless it is scriptural. The Holy Spirit wrote the Bible through anointed authors who were inspired of God, and He will never tell us to go against the Scriptures. We find this truth in Second Timothy 3:16: *"All scripture is given by inspiration of God, and is profitable for doctrine, for reproof, for correction, for instruction in righteousness."*

Contending in Prayer

As we prayed for my daughter that day, my friend Gwendolyn kept saying that we only needed to pray once and then believe God that He answered. Although there are times when you can pray in faith once and then rest in knowing the answers are on the way, there are also times when you need to contend. The Holy Spirit will let you know what to do by giving you a peace inside that the work is done or a heaviness that there is more to do in prayer. Luke 18:1-18 records a parable of Jesus where He encourages His disciples to pray and not quit: *"And he spake a parable unto them to this end, that men ought always to pray, and not to faint"* (Luke 18:1).

Jesus goes on to tell a story about a widow who persistently asked an unjust judge to avenge her. The judge finally gave her what she wanted lest she weary him. Jesus says in verses 7 and 8: *"And shall not God avenge His own elect, which cry day and night unto Him, though He bear long with them? I tell you that He will avenge them speedily."* Jesus shows us that Father God, who is just and good, is so much more attentive to our prayers than the unjust judge was to the woman. Even if it seems as if the answer is not coming, we are not to give up. Our promise is that God will answer us quickly.

We can see from this parable we should always pray and not faint, being confident God will answer us, but when the answer seems to be delayed, we often want to give up. This is why *praying through* until the burden is released is so important. Once we have peace inside, we can rest in faith whether we see the answer immediately or not.

The only way to really know how to pray effectively for each situation is to listen to the Holy Spirit speaking to you in your spirit. It is a knowing inside. Some ministers say that you know that you know that you know. When you are attentive to the Lord's leading, He *will* lead you. He promised He would and He does. The Lord wants to communicate with you.

And thine ears shall hear a word behind thee, saying, This is the way, walk ye in it, when ye turn to the right hand, and when you turn to the left (Isaiah 30:21).

Guidance in Decisions

God's guidance for us includes all the situations of our lives, especially the major decisions such as a career path or where to live. There is no Scripture that tells us exactly what to do, so we must rely on the Holy Spirit to lead us. My husband and I found ourselves in one of these instances in our early years.

My father-in-law was the founder and pastor of a church in Oregon. He passed away unexpectedly and the church requested my husband Wilbur and I come to pastor the church. Wilbur had family there but was already pastor of a church in South Dakota where my family was from. We were being pulled in both directions and really needed the Lord to make plain to us what to do. We prayed every day for a week and still did not have peace about the decision.

That Sunday I was not feeling well and stayed home from church. I felt led to look up all the Scriptures on guidance. I sat down and typed them out—one by one. By the time I was finished, I had a knowing in my spirit we were supposed to stay in South Dakota.

Wilbur came home from church and announced to me he knew we were not supposed to go to Oregon. God spoke the same thing to both of us in different ways. He made it clear what we were supposed to do.

In this case, we did not pray through in one sitting. It took longer for both of us to feel confident we had heard from God. We just kept the decision in prayer until God gave us the knowing of what to do. As the psalmist tells us: *"I will instruct thee and teach thee in the way which thou shalt go: I will guide thee with Mine eye"* (Ps. 32:8).

Continual Communication With God

You cannot put the Creator of the universe in a formula. It's by continual communication with the Lord that He leads you in prayer. By continual, I mean you converse with God every day and throughout your day. He wants to be involved in your life and will help you as often as you allow Him. Often, those in our prayer group who have a continual fellowship with the Lord will be led to pray certain ways. As you learn to hear God's leading inside, your prayer life will become more effective.

My sister Mary Ruth had a physical condition that was quite alarming. Her eyesight had begun to fade and she was unable to see to drive at night. In our prayer group, our friend Sharon felt led to pray specifically for Mary Ruth. We gathered around her, anointed her with oil, and laid hands on her according to the Scriptures in James, chapter 5.

Is any sick among you? let him call for the elders of the church; and let them pray over him, anointing him with oil in the name of the Lord: And the prayer of faith shall save the sick, and the Lord shall raise him up; and if he have committed sins, they shall be forgiven him (James 5:14-15).

Instantly, Mary Ruth could see clearly! Her eyes were bright again not only to her, but others could also see a change in her eyes. Sharon was guided by the Holy Spirit to pray that night for Mary Ruth. That type of guidance is the same as what we find in Isaiah 58:11:

And the LORD shall guide thee continually, and satisfy thy soul in drought, and make fat thy bones: and thou shalt be like a watered garden, and like a spring of water, whose waters fail not.

It is important you learn to listen inside to what God is speaking to you. Effective prayer is not one-sided—making your requests and hoping God answers. Instead, it is communication from both sides. It includes praising and worshiping Him, expressing your thanks for His goodness and blessings, making requests for His help, listening to what He tells you, and receiving His peace and joy. That sounds like a lot, but it is just the same as communicating with someone you love. You compliment the ones you love. You're thankful when they help you. You talk to them and they respond back. You get to know each other well because you communicate often. It is no different with God.

Psalm 100:4 tells us to *"Enter into His gates with thanksgiving and into His courts with praise:*

be thankful unto Him, and bless His holy name". Our praise and thanksgiving prepare our hearts to hear God's direction in our prayers. We not only make our requests to the Lord, but we listen to His response in our spirits.

Trust in the Lord

When you bring God into your life by engaging Him in your daily decisions, He can lead you and show you what to do. Proverbs 3:5-6 tells us to *"Trust in the LORD with all thine heart; and lean not unto thine own understanding. In all thy ways acknowledge Him and He shall direct thy paths."*

What we think in our natural mind is not always what is best for us. God can see into our future; He has a much better view of what we should do. They say hindsight is always 20/20, but we can have God's *forward* sight through prayer before we make decisions. We can expect God to lead us when we take the time to share our hearts with Him. God is big enough for the little things and the big things in our lives. And when we take joy in spending time with God, Psalm 37 tells us that the Lord will give us the desires of our hearts.

Trust in the LORD, and do good; so shalt thou dwell in the land, and verily thou shalt be fed. Delight thyself also in the LORD; and He shall give thee the desires of thine heart. Commit thy way unto the LORD; trust also in Him; and He shall bring it to pass (Psalm 37:3-5).

Praying in the Name of Jesus

Prayer is simply talking to the Lord, but we can pray more effectively by following the guidelines given to us in the Bible. In John 14:14 Jesus Himself told the disciples that if they would pray to the Father in His name, the Father would do what they requested. The disciples may not have understood this at the time because Jesus had not died on the cross yet, but they did understand after Jesus' resurrection. In the Book of Acts, they always prayed in Jesus' name.

Jesus Christ became our mediator to God when He died as an innocent man, a man without sin, and shed His blood for our sins. When we have a direct command like this in the Scripture, it's important to take note for our prayers to be effective. Always come to the Father in the name of Jesus when you make requests.

A Righteous Man

James 5:16 tells us that the fervent prayer of a righteous man makes great power available. You become a righteous man or woman when you are born again, no matter what sins you have committed. It is the greatest gift anyone could ever receive freedom through Jesus Christ. Find out more about this precious gift and the power it brings you in prayer in the next chapter.

Remember this:

- Listen to the Holy Spirit in your spirit.

- Pray through or pray until the burden lifts.

- The Holy Spirit always agrees with the Scriptures.

- The Lord wants to guide you and help you in all situations of life.

- Ask the Lord about your daily decisions.

- Pray in Jesus' name as the Scriptures tell us.

Chapter 2

The Most Important Things

Praying through is effective for the believer—someone whose spirit has been born again in Jesus Christ. Being sure you are a "believer" and your eternal home is in Heaven, is most important. Just a heart's cry for mercy and salvation will be heard by the Father in Heaven. The Scriptures tell us that *"Whosoever shall call upon the name of the Lord shall be saved"* (Rom. 10:13). No particular words need to be used; you just need a sincere heart.

The assurance of salvation is defined in Romans 8:16 where it shows the Holy Spirit bears witness with our spirit that we are the children of God. This is an inner witness not an outward feeling, and no one can take it away from you. When you give your heart to the Lord, you don't have to feel anything because you take salvation by faith.

You just believe, but it is always nice when you feel something. Everyone's experience with salvation is unique and personal, but the Lord Jesus Christ is the same yesterday, today, and forever (see Heb. 13:8).

Any Time Is a Good Time to Pray

I was about five years old when I gave my heart to the Lord. It was on a Sunday morning. I can remember where it happened: by the chair, second row from the front in the middle section in our church. My husband was twelve years old when he walked down the aisle in a theater used for evangelistic meetings. He and his cousin went together, and their fathers came and prayed with them. My own father was 88 years old when he prayed the prayer of salvation. Any age or any time you reach out to the Lord, you can be saved.

Jesus Tells of Salvation

The best chapter in the Bible to understand salvation is John, chapter 3. It would benefit you greatly to read and even more to memorize it. Jesus shares with a man named Nicodemus, a Pharisee or religious leader of that time. He tells Nicodemus that a man must be born of the flesh and of the Spirit to see the Kingdom of God. In fact, Jesus even shares with Nicodemus that He, Jesus, would have to die on the cross and whoever believes in Him will have eternal life. In John 3:14-17 we read what Nicodemus heard:

And as Moses lifted up the serpent in the wilderness, even so must the Son of man be lifted up: That whosoever believeth in Him should not perish, but have eternal life. For God so loved the world, that He gave His only begotten Son, that whosoever believeth in Him should not perish, but have everlasting life. For God sent not His Son into the world to condemn the world; but that the world through Him might be saved.

You can receive Jesus Christ as your Savior and begin an amazing relationship with Him right now. Your life will never be the same. You might use the following prayer as a guide:

Father God, I confess that I am a sinner, but today I believe the Lord Jesus Christ died on the cross for my sins, and He was raised from the dead for my justification. I receive and confess Him as my personal Savior.

You can sign your name and the date you prayed this prayer in the back of this book. That way, if the enemy ever comes and threatens you about your eternal destiny, you can always remember this day and be confident Jesus is your Lord.

Prayer Is a Privilege

Because Jesus died for us, one of the amazing privileges He gave us is that we can enter the throne room of the great Creator of the whole universe without an appointment at any time of the day or night. When we receive Jesus as our Lord, His blood covers our sins, and the Father God sees us as holy and righteous no matter what our past has been. Our sins are forgiven. The Father God wants to talk with us, and Jesus has made a way for us to come to Him.

I have always loved and trusted Jesus, but I was afraid of God the Father. One night while in prayer, Jesus said to me, "I want you to go into the throne room of my Father and tell Him your prayer requests." In my spirit I saw myself go into the throne room, but once I was there, all I could see was mist. I was afraid and I could not say a word. The vision left me.

The next night Jesus again said to me, "Go into my Father's throne room and tell Him what you want." Again, I was too afraid to say a word. On the third night, I went into the throne room and hastily recited all my requests and then ran out again. Ever since then, I have not been afraid of my heavenly Father. In fact, I love to talk to Him, and He answers me when I listen to Him.

Forgiveness in Christ

Another amazing privilege we have as believers is forgiveness when we make mistakes. First John 1:9 tells us, *"If we confess our sins, He is faithful and just to forgive us our sins, and to cleanse us from all unrighteousness."*

When you give your life to the Lord Jesus, you bring your load of sin to the cross and leave it there. You do not have to name every sin you have done; but after you are a Christian, you name your sins and ask forgiveness. You will not have so many sins that you cannot name them. Isaiah 59:12 tells us, *"...as for our iniquities, we know them."*

The Holy Spirit will convict you in your spirit and you will know that you need to repent. To repent means that you change directions and no longer do those things. After you make a commitment to serve the Lord and repent, you are forgiven. Isaiah 43:25 reminds us, "I, even I, am He that blotteth out thy transgressions for Mine own sake, and will not remember thy sins."

As holocaust survivor Corrie Ten Boom says in her book *Tramp for the Lord:* God puts your sins in the sea of His forgetfulness and puts up a sign, "NO FISHING ALLOWED".[1]

The Power of Praying in the Spirit

I have found that praying in the Spirit is so valuable in praying through. In the Bible, this is also called praying in tongues. When my daughter was in trouble and the Lord gave Gwendolyn, Mary Ruth, and me a burden to pray for her, we didn't know exactly how to pray or what the specific need was. As we prayed in the Spirit—or to say it another way, as we "prayed in tongues,"—the Holy Spirit led us in a heavenly language we did not completely understand in our natural minds, but it was the perfect prayer for the situation at hand. The apostle Paul's letter to the Romans says:

Likewise the Spirit also helpeth our infirmities: for we know not what we should pray for as we ought: but the Spirit itself maketh intercession for us with groanings which cannot be uttered.

And He that searcheth the hearts knoweth what is the mind of the Spirit, because He maketh intercession for the saints according to the will of God.

And we know that all things work together for good to them that love God, to them who are the called according to His purpose (Romans 8:26-28).

Part of the work of the Holy Spirit is to help His children pray the prayer needed to accomplish the will of God in the earth. The Lord seemingly limits what He does on the earth to the prayers of believers. We need to take time to pray in the Spirit to get this work accomplished.

The Holy Spirit is a gentleman and does not assist you without your permission. If you welcome Him and follow His leading, you will do great things in prayer. You may never know—until the rewards are handed out in Heaven—what wonderful feats you accomplished from praying according to God's will.

Receiving the Power of the Holy Spirit

The first two chapters of the Book of Acts introduce us wonderfully to Jesus' command to receive the power of the Holy Spirit.

*And, being assembled together with them, commanded **them** that they should not depart from Jerusalem, but wait for the promise of the Father, which, saith He, ye have heard of Me.*

For John truly baptized with water; but ye shall be baptized with the Holy Ghost not many days hence.

When they therefore were come together, they asked of Him, saying, Lord, wilt thou at this time restore again the kingdom to Israel?

And He said unto them, It is not for you to know the times or the seasons, which the Father hath put in His own power.

But ye shall receive power, after that the Holy Ghost is come upon you: and ye shall be witnesses unto Me both in Jerusalem, and in all Judaea, and in Samaria, and unto the uttermost part of the earth (Acts 1:4-8, emphasis added).

The disciples' first experience with the Holy Spirit after Jesus was taken up into Heaven is told in Acts 2:1-4:

And when the day of Pentecost was fully come, they were all with one accord in one place.

And suddenly there came a sound from heaven as of a rushing mighty wind, and it filled all the house where they were sitting.

And there appeared unto them cloven tongues like as of fire, and it sat upon each of them.

And they were all filled with the Holy Ghost, and began to speak with other tongues, as the Spirit gave them utterance.

Everyone Can Receive

When the disciples received the Holy Spirit, the evidence was their speaking in an unknown language as the Spirit led them. This is often referred to as "praying in the Spirit" or "being filled with the Spirit." As you can imagine, when the people of Jerusalem heard the disciples speaking in tongues, it caused a great commotion, and many rushed over to them to find out what was going on. Peter, inspired by the Holy Spirit, spoke to the crowd about Jesus, and many were convicted of their sins. Peter told them what they should do in Acts 2:37-39. We learn in this passage that everyone who is saved can receive the power of the Holy Spirit, not just the disciples.

Now when they heard this, they were pricked in their heart, and said unto Peter and to the rest of the apostles, Men and brethren, what shall we do?

Then Peter said unto them, Repent, and be baptized every one of you in the name of Jesus Christ for the remission of sins, and ye shall receive the gift of the Holy Ghost.

For the promise is unto you, and to your children, and to all that are afar off, even as many as the LORD our God shall call (Acts 2:37-39).

During Peter's first sermon, he also quotes an Old Testament reference where the prophet Joel foretells of the coming of the Holy Spirit. In Acts 2:16 Peter declares, *"But this is that which was spoken by the prophet Joel...."*

And it shall come to pass afterward, that I will pour out My spirit upon all flesh; and your sons and your daughters shall prophesy, your old men shall dream dreams, your young men shall see visions: And also upon the servants and upon the handmaids in those days will I pour out My spirit (Joel 2:28-29).

In Acts chapter 10 the Lord gives Peter a vision letting him know that the Gentiles as well as the Jews are allowed to hear the Gospel and be filled with the Holy Spirit. Peter is preaching the Gospel of Jesus Christ in Cornelius's home. Cornelius was a Gentile and not a Jew; he and those with him were all filled with the Holy Spirit.

While Peter yet spake these words, the Holy Ghost fell on all them which heard the word.

And they of the circumcision which believed were astonished, as many as came with Peter, because that on the Gentiles also was poured out the gift of the Holy Ghost.

For they heard them speak with tongues, and magnify God. Then answered Peter,

Can any man forbid water, that these should not be baptized, which have received the Holy Ghost as well as we?

And he commanded them to be baptized in the name of the Lord. Then prayed they him to tarry certain days (Acts 10:44-48).

People who have not received the fullness of the Holy Spirit with the evidence of speaking in tongues can pray through, but it is more difficult. Pray the Scripture promises that pertain to your situation back to the Father God; personalize these Scripture promises, and declare them as yours. Praying the Scriptures is effective for every believer, but I have found there were times when I just did not know what to pray in my own understanding. I needed the power of praying in the Spirit.

Filled to Overflowing

This wonderful gift of speaking in tongues is also called the "baptism of the Holy Spirit." However, different denominations have used the term *baptism* as water baptism for infants, and others use it as well for various experiences. To clarify the work of the Holy Spirit, you need to know that when you are saved, you receive the Holy Spirit, but when you are "filled" in the Holy Spirit, you are filled to overflowing with the evidence of speaking in tongues.

In Acts chapter 2, the disciples prayed in tongues when they received the Holy Spirit. When it comes to *praying through*, it is so important to use this gift. It truly allows the Holy Spirit to pray that perfect prayer through you and gives you additional wisdom to know how to pray in your understanding as well.

You Don't Need to Wait

I grew up in a Pentecostal church; we were taught that you needed to "tarry" until you received the gift of speaking in tongues. At that time, we believed we were doing just as the disciples had done—waiting for the Holy Spirit to come. But now, the Holy Spirit is here. We do not need to tarry anymore. We can receive Him at any time.

When the Charismatic movement swept America in the 1970s, my husband Wilbur and I took carloads of people to Omaha to hear the speakers brought in by Full Gospel Businessmen's Fellowship. One night I observed the speaker praying for people; they immediately received the baptism of the Holy Spirit with the evidence of speaking in tongues. I went home and prayed for people the same way and they received without "tarrying." We were thrilled to see God moving like that, but many in our church did not like it. We were persecuted, but we chose to move with the Spirit of God. We have no regrets and were so blessed to see many people filled with the Holy Spirit.

Just Ask

You can receive this wonderful gift too. You just have to ask and the Lord will gladly give it to you.

If a son shall ask bread of any of you that is a father, will he give him a stone? or if he ask a fish, will he for a fish give him a serpent?

Or if he shall ask an egg, will he offer him a scorpion?

If ye then, being evil, know how to give good gifts unto your children: how much more shall your heavenly Father give the Holy Spirit to them that ask him? (Luke 11:11-13)

I prayed for several years as a young woman to receive the baptism of the Holy Spirit, but there was no one there to help me. I was dating an unsaved young man at the time, and every time I would pray about the baptism, I just had a knowing that I should not be dating him.

During my first year at Central Bible College, I got serious about receiving this wonderful gift. I finally told the Lord that I would break off the relationship with that man and I did. The very next day I attended a revival meeting with a busload of my classmates at a local church. When they gave the altar call to receive the Holy Spirit, I went down. Many people gathered around me and prayed. A friend from school said, "You have to get those lightning rods up!" and pushed both of my arms up. This was very uncomfortable for me since I never lifted my hands in church. I wanted to hide my face so no one could see what I was praying.

Another classmate kept saying, "Praise the Lord" while spitting in my face, but I was determined to receive. I saw a vision in my spirit of going up stairs. The higher I went, the stronger the light shown. At the top I began singing in tongues to the tune, "Blessed Be the Tie That Binds." When I finally opened my eyes, almost everyone had left, and I felt sorry I kept my busload from going back to Bible school. But I was thrilled to have received the gift of speaking in tongues.

When I got back to my room, I woke my roommate to tell her the good news. She was so irritated that I woke her up and didn't share my enthusiasm. I have noticed when you get something from the Lord not everyone wants to hear about it. There is often someone who will throw a wet blanket on your experience because the enemy wants to stop this wonderful gift. Don't allow anyone to steal your joy about the good things God does for you.

You Can Receive Now

To receive the baptism of the Holy Spirit with the evidence of speaking in tongues, just ask. If you are convicted that there is sin in your life, then repent. It's good to thank the Lord for His wonderful gift, too. Then take a deep breath; let the Holy Spirit use your tongue. He uses your voice and your tongue to speak a different language. The Holy Spirit does not "zap" you and you are not out of control. You simply yield your voice to His leading. You do the speaking and He gives you the words. You may want to use this prayer to receive the infilling of the Holy Spirit:

Father God, In Jesus' name I ask you to fill me with the Holy Spirit with the evidence of speaking in tongues. I repent of all my sins. Thank you for this wonderful gift.

Now take a deep breath and start speaking in another language. You may receive immediately or you may need to just start praising the Lord. Do not give up. God wants you to have this powerful gift.

I was so excited to have the gift of speaking in tongues. I used it as much as possible. I also sang in the Spirit frequently. In fact, I couldn't sing very well before or hear harmony until after I sang in tongues so much. Speaking in tongues and praying in the Spirit are the same, just as are singing in the Spirit and singing in tongues. Paul explains this in his letter to the Corinthians:

"What is it then? I will pray with the spirit, and I will pray with the understanding also: I will sing with the spirit, and I will sing with the understanding also" (1 Corinthians 14:15).

Pray in Tongues Often

After you receive the gift of speaking in tongues, be sure to use it often. In Jude verse 20, the Scriptures tell us that praying in the Spirit builds up our most holy faith. The very act of praying in tongues takes faith and builds your faith. It may not make sense to your natural mind, but when you take time to pray in tongues, things around you will begin to change in your favor. That builds your faith in God and in knowing that His Word works. The book of Jude explains it like this: *"But ye, beloved, building up yourselves on your most holy faith, praying in the Holy Ghost"* (Jude 1:20).

As a young girl I was taught that you could not pray in tongues unless you were "in the Spirit" or caught up in some kind of supernatural move of

God. From Revelation 1:10, our church leadership deduced that since the apostle John was "in the Spirit" on the Lord's day, we had to be as well. This hindered many believers from speaking in tongues unless they were in a powerful meeting where the Spirit of the Lord was moving. But the apostle Paul declared in First Corinthians 14:18, *"I thank my God, I speak with tongues more than ye all."*

It is almost impossible to pray for very long in your own language, but you can pray in tongues for hours. My husband Wilbur and I have done this in certain situations for up to eight hours at a time with only a lunch break. The results have always been very positive.

Speaking Mysteries Brings Revelation

First Corinthians 14:2 and 4 tell us that when we speak in tongues, we speak mysteries and it brings revelation to us. This may be revelation about natural things or spiritual things. You can receive more revelation from reading the Word of God with the power of the Holy Spirit helping you. It also says that praying in tongues edifies you. That means you are encouraged and built up in your inner-being:

*For he that speaketh in an unknown tongue
speaketh not unto men, but unto God: for no
man understandeth him; howbeit in the spirit
he speaketh mysteries...He that speaketh
in an unknown tongue edifieth himself...*
(1 Corinthians 14:2,4).

Once, I was traveling to a meeting and I was
worshiping the Lord and singing in tongues. During that time, I was driving through a beautiful valley with a river running through it. I asked the Lord
what I was saying and He answered me by allowing
me to sing the interpretation. In my song, He was
telling me how much He enjoyed my appreciation
of the beauty of His creation. I never realized that
it was important to the Father God for me to enjoy
nature. This was a mystery that was revealed to me
by singing in the Spirit.

Intercession for Others

Ephesians 6:18-19 shows us another example
of praying in the Spirit. In this instance, we are
admonished to pray in the Spirit in relationship to
praying for others. Paul desired the Ephesians to
pray in the Spirit for him that he would have boldness to preach the Gospel:

*Praying always with all prayer and suppli-
cation in the Spirit, and watching thereunto
with all perseverance and supplication for all
saints;*

*And for me, that utterance may be given unto
me, that I may open my mouth boldly, to make
known the mystery of the gospel* (Ephesians
6:18-19).

We also need boldness when God gives us the
opportunity to preach the Gospel, and praying in
the Spirit can help us in this area.

I know a missionary who was traveling in Central
America. One morning as he left his hotel, several
robbers jumped him and beat him. He was miracu-
lously able to escape them. He later found out that
a lady in Michigan was burdened to pray for him
at that exact hour. She had written down the date
and time. When they compared notes, they realized that prayer had saved his life. She was praying
as the Holy Spirit led her. Praise God she took the
time to pray through!

Praying the Will of God

Many times you really do not know what to pray,
but you can always pray in tongues and know you

are praying the perfect prayer. The Scriptures tell us in Romans 8:26-27 that the Spirit helps us by making intercession for us according to the will of God:

Likewise the Spirit also helpeth our infirmities: for we know not what we should pray for as we ought: but the Spirit itself maketh intercession for us with groanings which cannot be uttered.

And He that searcheth the hearts knoweth what is the mind of the Spirit, because He maketh intercession for the saints according to the will of God (Romans 8:26-27).

The Holy Spirit makes intercession through us when we pray in the Spirit. It is an amazing blessing that we can pray exactly what needs to be prayed over our lives and the lives of others by praying in tongues.

Standing in the Gap

In intercession, or praying for others, you are the link between the Lord and the person you are praying about. Ezekiel 22:30 relates an incident when the nation of Israel was lost because there was no one to stand in the gap or no one to pray and make intercession for the protection and redemption of the people. That was in the Old Testament, but we live under the New Testament, and the Holy Spirit has come. Any believer can stand in the gap for others by praying in the Spirit and praying through.

After you have prayed, Romans 8:28 says that all things will work for good. Even if bad things have happened, the genius of the Lord is to get some good out of it: *"And we know that all things work together for good to them that love God, to them who are the called according to his purpose"* (Rom. 8:28).

Conformed to His Image

The next verse, Romans 8:29, tells us of another work of the Holy Spirit to make us look like Jesus, "conformed to the image of Christ." As we get to know the Holy Spirit through praying in the Spirit and talking with Him, He helps us live like Jesus. Things that you may have struggled with, He helps you to overcome. Again, the apostle Paul writes: *"For whom He did foreknow, He also did predestinate to be conformed to the image of His Son, that He might be the firstborn among many brethren"* (Rom. 8:29).

Verse 30 shows us that we are called by God, justified by God, and glorified! Even though we are not perfect, God sees us as glorified and justified: *"Moreover whom He did predestinate, them He also called: and whom He called, them He also justified: and whom He justified, them He also glorified"* (Rom. 8:30).

Romans 8:31 says that if God be for us, who can be against us? What a promise that is! In verse 32 we discover that since the Father gave us Jesus, He will also give us all things. It almost sounds too good to be true, but it is true. God loves us so much He made it possible for us to live in victory not just when we get to Heaven, but right now. Read these verses for yourself:

> *What shall we then say to these things? If God be for us, who can be against us? He that spared not His own Son, but delivered Him up for us all, how shall He not with Him also freely give us all things?* (Romans 8:31-32)

Nothing Can Separate You From God's Love

Romans 8:35-38 goes on to tell us that nothing can separate us from the love of God. There is a list

of things that you might think could separate us
from the love of God, but they cannot.

> *Who shall separate us from the love of Christ?*
> *shall tribulation, or distress, or persecution, or*
> *famine, or nakedness, or peril, or sword?*
>
> *As it is written, For Thy sake we are killed all*
> *the day long; we are accounted as sheep for*
> *the slaughter.*
>
> *Nay, in all these things we are more than*
> *conquerors through Him that loved us.*
>
> *For I am persuaded, that neither death, nor*
> *life, nor angels, nor principalities, nor powers,*
> *nor things present, nor things to come,*
>
> *Nor height, nor depth, nor any other creature,*
> *shall be able to separate us from the love*
> *of God, which is in Christ Jesus our Lord*
> (Romans 8:35-39).

Your Prayer Language Can Change

As you pray in tongues the language will change
from time to time. The intensity will also change according to the need. Your tongues could be praise
or intercession or warfare or for the needs you have

personally. Often you can tell by the tone and how you feel in your inner being. If you want to know what you are praying, just ask the Lord and often the Holy Spirit will tell you. It will probably not be an audible voice, but a knowing in your spirit.

Three Kinds of Tongues

There are three kinds of tongues mentioned in the Bible. First, in Acts 2:8-11, we are told of tongues as being known languages of other groups that were present. The crowd that had gathered when they heard the disciples speaking in tongues recognized and understood what the disciples were praying out in the Spirit.

Second, in First Corinthians 13:1, there are tongues of men and angels. I believe "tongues of men" refers to the various languages spoken by people throughout the earth. Tongues of angels, however, are not given an explanation in the Scriptures. But apparently angels have certain languages as well.

Third, in First Corinthians 14:2-4, there are unknown languages that we speak to God as we speak in tongues. The Holy Spirit can use any of the three types of languages when you yield yourself to Him to pray in the Spirit since He knows what needs to be prayed. I have experienced many different variations of tongues as I have prayed over the years. Once I was praying in the Spirit and my mouth opened very wide. I was curious about this strange language and I asked the Holy Spirit about it. He told me I was praying in the tongues of angels.

There are many other Scriptures that foretell of the coming of the Holy Spirit in the Old Testament and the New. For further study, please refer to the Appendix in the back of this book.

Effective Prayer

To have an effective prayer life, I cannot stress enough the importance of receiving the baptism of the Holy Spirit with the evidence of speaking with other tongues. The Holy Spirit has also given us many other gifts that are important in praying through. We will discuss them in the next chapter.

Remember this:

- You must be saved to pray effectively.

- Praying in tongues is important in praying through.

- You can receive this gift just by asking God.

- Pray in tongues often and build your most holy faith.

- Pray in tongues when you don't know what to pray.

Endnote

1. Corrie Ten Boom, *Tramp for the Lord* (Christian Literature Crusade, 2008).

Chapter 3

Revelation Gifts

On a sunny day in May during the planting season, my husband Wilbur was working in the shop. The corn planter had broken down; he was welding it back together. Wilbur farmed and at various times throughout his career simultaneously served as a pastor. His time was valuable; it was important to get the planter up and running to get the seed planted.

Just then a salesman drove into the yard. The Holy Spirit spoke to Wilbur in his spirit and told him the salesman was hurting. Wilbur thought, "Yes Lord, a lot of people are hurting." The salesman, Ron, introduced himself and offered Wilbur some farm tools. Wilbur told him that he was busy right then and asked if he could come back in two weeks. But the Lord persisted by saying to Wilbur, "If you don't buy something from him, how will you tell him about Me?" Wilbur said to Ron, "Well, I could take some welding rods and hacksaw blades." Wilbur thanked him and said, "Ron, have you ever made a commitment to the Lord?" Ron replied, "No, I haven't."

"Would you like to?" asked Wilbur.

Ron said, "Yes, I would."

Wilbur pulled out a little Gideon New Testament that he always kept handy. They read the salvation Scriptures and the prayer to receive Jesus as Lord written in the back. Ron signed his name and the date in the blank spaces provided for just such a time.

Then Ron said, "I have been reading the Bible all winter and it never made any sense to me, but you made it so plain."

Ron drove away a changed man, but it would not have happened if the Lord had not given Wilbur some help.

In this instance, Wilbur received and used several of the gifts of the Spirit found in First Corinthians 12 to help lead Ron to the Lord. A word of knowledge from the Lord let him know Ron was hurting. Wilbur also received a word of wisdom that instructed him to buy something from Ron and prompted him to ask Ron if he had made a commitment to the Lord. It also took a gift of faith for Wilbur to step out and boldly witness to Ron. These gifts are outlined for us very clearly in the Scriptures.

Now there are diversities of gifts, but the same Spirit.

And there are differences of administrations, but the same Lord.

And there are diversities of operations, but it is the same God which worketh all in all.

But the manifestation of the Spirit is given to every man to profit withal.

For to one is given by the Spirit the word of wisdom; to another the word of knowledge by the same Spirit;

To another faith by the same Spirit; to another the gifts of healing by the same Spirit;

To another the working of miracles; to another prophecy; to another discerning of spirits; to another divers kinds of tongues; to another the interpretation of tongues:

But all these worketh that one and the selfsame Spirit, dividing to every man severally as he will (1 Corinthians 12:4-11).

The gifts of the Holy Spirit are especially needed in praying through. These gifts work together just like the colors of a rainbow and help you know how to receive the answers to your prayers. The nine gifts of the Holy Spirit are: the word of wisdom, the word of knowledge, the gift of faith, the gifts of healing, the working of miracles, prophecy, discerning of spirits, different kinds of tongues, and interpretation of tongues. You can divide these gifts into three different groups in order to understand them better:

The Revelation Gifts

- The word of wisdom

- The word of knowledge

- Discerning of spirits

The Vocal Gifts

- Prophecy

- Different kinds of tongues

- The interpretation of tongues

The Power Gifts

- The gift of faith

- The gifts of healing

- The working of miracles

The Lord has other gifts and talents that He gives as well, but these gifts of the Spirit are mentioned specifically to help us live in the power and revelation of God every day. They are not just for certain people. They are for everyone. In First Corinthians 13 God makes a very strong statement that these gifts are worthless without love. They are not meant to control people; they are meant to be a blessing. When we work with the Holy Spirit, these gifts can effect amazing change in people's lives, including your own. God also gives us guidance on how to use these gifts in First Corinthians 14.

The Revelation Gifts: The Word of Wisdom

When Wilbur was prompted by the Lord to ask Ron if he had ever made a commitment to the Lord, the word of wisdom was needed especially because so little was said. But it was just enough. Ron was ready to receive the Lord. He did not need anyone to talk him into it because the Holy Spirit had already dealt with his heart. In fact, within a month Ron had received the baptism in the Holy Spirit with the evidence of speaking in tongues as well.

A word of wisdom lets you know about a future event or instructs you what to do in your future. In Wilbur's case, the event was only a few seconds away, but the Lord gave him wisdom regarding what to do. The word of wisdom is given in many different situations. The Holy Spirit may give this gift to you as a warning in order for you to pray or prepare. This gift could also be given when you need to know what to say or do in certain difficult situations. And it is often needed when you are witnessing or leading someone to the Lord.

On a winter evening while our son was in college, Wilbur and I were attending a candlelight wedding. The Holy Spirit spoke a word of wisdom to me in my spirit during the ceremony and told me our son would be in a car accident. We were sitting in the back of the church so I plead the blood of Jesus Christ and prayed in tongues as best I could. A phone call came a few hours later—our son had hit an ice patch and wrecked his car. Both he and his friend were all right. The impact threw our son into the windshield, but the injuries were minor. Praise the Lord for His wonderful gift that warned me to pray.

In another situation, the word of wisdom came to my friend Gwendolyn as a vision. My sister Mary Ruth and I were praying with Gwendolyn when she saw a vision of Mary Ruth's son on water skis. At that time her son lived in another state. In the vision there was a dark, evil circle around his waist. We instantly knew that he was in danger and we prayed until we prayed through. Later we found out that he was water skiing that day and had almost drowned! His girlfriend thought he was dead when they pulled him into the boat, but he recovered completely.

Jesus used the word of wisdom in His ministry. We can read an example in Matthew chapter 9:

And when Jesus came into the ruler's house, and saw the minstrels and the people making a noise, He said unto them, Give place; for the maid is not dead, but sleepeth. And they laughed Him to scorn. But when the people were put forth, He went in, and took her by the hand, and the maid arose (Matthew 9:23-25).

When Jesus tells the people that the maid is not dead, He is operating in the word of wisdom. The Holy Spirit lets Him know the maid will be raised from the dead.

The word of wisdom may come to you as a knowing, a vision, or even a dream. When God speaks to you this way, it is for a reason. It may be a warning to pray through, or it may be confirmation of a decision or direction for your life. Whenever you receive a word of wisdom, pray about it and let God lead you. If you receive a warning, pray right away.

The Lord gives you a warning because He needs you to take action. Pray and follow His direction.

The Revelation Gifts: The Word of Knowledge

A word of knowledge is when the Holy Spirit tells you something you would not know in the natural about a current situation. It would be supernatural knowledge. When you receive this gift, it does not mean you have supernatural knowledge about everything or that you have it all the time. God gives it to you only when it is needed.

My sister Mary Ruth lived across the road from our farm and often came over in the mornings. Our usual routine was to take a walk, then have coffee and pray for our families. On one particular morning she came over quite early. She had a disturbing dream about her son and my youngest son. In the dream, they were in a cabin together, starving to death. Her son lived in Washington at that time and my son was at home and in grade school.

After a time of prayer, Mary Ruth and I both felt the dream must have been a warning about spiritual starvation. This revelation was a word of knowledge about a current situation. We prayed until the burden lifted: we prayed through. We could see the change in my youngest son because he lived with us. His attitude toward spiritual things changed after that. We believed in faith for the change in Mary Ruth's son since he lived so far away, but time has revealed that our prayers made a difference in his life as well. The word of knowledge is such a powerful gift in your prayer life. What a blessing it is to be able to pray accurately by the leading of the Holy Spirit.

Jesus uses the word of knowledge in the first part of Matthew, chapter 9. The Scripture tells us Jesus knew the thoughts of those who were criticizing him. That kind of supernatural knowing is the word of knowledge as displayed in the following verses:

And He entered into a ship, and passed over, and came into His own city. And, behold, they brought to Him a man sick of the palsy, lying on a bed: and Jesus seeing their faith said unto the sick of the palsy; Son, be of good cheer; thy sins be forgiven thee. And, behold, certain of the scribes said within themselves, This man blasphemeth. And Jesus knowing their thoughts said, Wherefore think ye evil in your hearts? For whether is easier, to say, Thy sins be forgiven thee; or to say, Arise, and walk? But that ye may know that the Son of man hath power on earth to forgive sins, (then saith He to the sick of the palsy,) Arise, take up thy bed, and go unto thine house. And he arose, and departed to his house (Matthew 9:1-7).

Testing the Spirits

I have operated in the word of knowledge for many years and often people call me for prayer. The Lord gives me a word of knowledge when I ask. It comes like a prophecy. The Lord gives me the thoughts. As I speak them out, I receive more. They must, of course, be judged by the person and must agree with the Scriptures. One of the ways to test a word from the Lord is mentioned in First John 4:1-4:

Beloved, believe not every spirit, but try the spirits whether they are of God: because many false prophets are gone out into the world.

Hereby know ye the Spirit of God: Every spirit that confesseth that Jesus Christ is come in the flesh is of God:

And every spirit that confesseth not that Jesus Christ is come in the flesh is not of God:

and this is that spirit of antichrist, whereof ye have heard that it should come; and even now already is it in the world.

Ye are of God, little children, and have overcome them: because greater is he that is in you, than he that is in the world.

The enemy can try to deceive you in this area and some words of knowledge need to be "tried" or "tested" to make sure they are from God and not a deceiving spirit from the enemy. To try or test a word of knowledge, ask the spirit that told you the word to say, "Jesus is come in the flesh." If the spirit says, "Yes," it is the Holy Spirit. If the spirit says, "No," the message is not from the Lord, but from the enemy. Even an evil spirit will obey you when you ask. It has to obey, because you have spiritual authority over evil spirits in the name of Jesus Christ.

It is important to know Jesus came in the flesh as a man. When God created the earth and gave the dominion to Adam (see Gen. 1:28), He gave Adam authority over all the creatures in the earth. The only way that Jesus would have a legal right to die for our sins is to come as a man and have authority in the earth. Evil spirits do not want to admit that Jesus came in the flesh because that would be admitting that He has authority over them and has defeated them.

The peace in your heart is another way to test a word. The enemy cannot imitate peace—only God can give you peace. Colossians 3:15 tells us of the peace of God, *"and let the peace of God rule in your hearts..."* And again in James 3:17 we find that peace is a good test:

> But the wisdom that is from above is first pure, then peaceable, gentle, and easy to be intreated, full of mercy and good fruits, without partiality, and without hypocrisy.

The Revelation Gifts: Discerning of Spirits

Discerning of spirits, the last revelation gift, is the ability to know what evil spirits are working in the situation you are praying about. This gift has been invaluable in my prayer ministry because it has helped so many people. Don't be afraid of this gift. The Holy Spirit gives it to us because we need it. Jesus dealt with evil spirits many times and has given us that same authority.

Evil spirits could also be called "demons" or even "attitudes." That doesn't mean every negative attitude is a spirit, but that some attitudes are caused by a spirit's influence. People seem to be more comfortable using the word *spirit* instead of *demon* because that word often scares them.

Satan or the devil is not like God. God is omnipresent, omnipotent, omniscient, and eternal. *Omnipotent* means He is all powerful. *Omnipresent* means He is everywhere at once. *Omniscient* means He is all-knowing. Satan, on the other hand, is not any of those things. He cannot be everywhere at once, so he has demons to do his work. Satan is not all-powerful. John 10:10 says that the thief (satan) comes to steal, to kill, and to destroy. He cannot create, only destroy; and he was defeated by Jesus Christ. Jesus took the keys of death and the grave away from satan when He was resurrected. We find this in Revelation 1:18: *"I [Jesus] am He that liveth, and was dead; and, behold, I am alive for evermore, Amen; and have the keys of hell and of death."*

We also read in Colossians 2:15 that Jesus spoiled all principalities and powers. Jesus spoiled all the weapons the devil had set against us:

> *[God] disarmed the principalities and powers that were ranged against us and made a bold display and public example of them, in triumphing over them in Him and in it [the cross]* (Colossians 2:15 AMP).

We discover in Ephesians that Jesus is far above any authority in this world or the world to come. The Scriptures tell us that all things are under the feet of Jesus (see 1 Cor. 15:27). And He is the head of the Church, His Body. That means all believers, as part of the Body of Christ, have all things under their feet, including the power of satan:

> [Power] *which He* [God] *wrought in Christ, when He raised Him from the dead, and set Him at His own right hand in the heavenly places,*
>
> *Far above all principality, and power, and might, and dominion, and every name that is named, not only in this world, but also in that which is to come:*
>
> *And hath put all things under His feet, and gave Him to be the head over all things to the church,*
>
> *Which is His body, the fulness of Him that filleth all in all* (Ephesians 1:20-23).

We have established that we have authority over satan because of Jesus Christ. Remember that God is all-knowing, lives inside of us, and can reveal supernatural knowledge to us.

Satan, however, is not all-knowing or omniscient as shown in First Corinthians 2:8. In this passage we see that the rulers of the world who crucified

Jesus would not have done so if they had known He was the Lord of Glory sent to redeem humankind. Whether those rulers were satan and his demons or the humans they influenced, in either case, satan sealed his doom when he crucified Jesus:

> But rather what we are setting forth is a wisdom of God once hidden [from the human understanding] and now revealed to us by God—[that wisdom] which God devised and decreed before the ages for our glorification [to lift us into the glory of His presence].
>
> None of the rulers of this age or world perceived and recognized and understood this, for if they had, they would never have crucified the Lord of glory (1 Corinthians 2:7-8 AMP).

Satan will live eternally, but eternally in hell according to Matthew 25 where Jesus is telling the parable of the sheep and the goats: *"Then He will say to those on His left, 'Depart from me, you who are cursed, into the eternal fire prepared for the devil and his angels'"* (Matt. 25:41 NIV).

Authority to Bind and Loose

When the gift of discerning of spirits is in operation, God gives you a knowing of what evil spirits are working in a certain situation. Once you know the spirit or spirits that are causing trouble, you can bind them away from that situation or person. You can't bind the devil or demons away from the whole world, only from the specific situation you are praying about. When you bind a demon, it stops him from working in that situation. This specific knowledge helps you to pinpoint your prayers and stop evil spirits from influencing others. Jesus gives us the authority to bind and lose spirits in the following Scriptures:

> ...say unto you, Whatsoever ye shall bind on earth shall be bound in heaven: and whatsoever ye shall loose on earth shall be loosed in heaven.
>
> Again I say unto you, That if two of you shall agree on earth as touching any thing that they shall ask, it shall be done for them of My Father which is in heaven (Matthew 18:18-19).

You bind evil spirits in the name of Jesus Christ, but you can't cast evil spirits out of a person without that person's permission. We will talk more about casting out demons in a later chapter. It is very important, however, in any of your prayers, to pray in the name of "Jesus Christ" as Jesus Himself tells us in the Book of John: *"And whatsoever ye shall ask in my name, that will I do, that the Father may be glorified in the Son. If ye shall ask any thing in my name, I will do it"* (John 14:13-14).

In the late 1970s I heard a speaker at an Aglow meeting who knew how to cast out devils. I wanted to know more about how she did this and specifically how she knew what spirit was operating in the people she prayed for. The gift she was flowing in was the discerning of spirits. She told me that when she asked the Lord what spirit was involved, the Lord would give her one word, which was the name of the spirit or what that spirit did. It would come right to her mind in a strong way, which she could recognize immediately. I began to do the same thing in my own prayer life, and the Lord would reveal the name of the evil spirit to me in much the same way. We find in the Scriptures that Jesus knew the names of demons and cast them out by their names as described in Mark 9:25-27:

> *When Jesus saw that the people came running together, He rebuked the foul spirit, saying unto him, Thou dumb and deaf spirit, I charge thee, come out of him, and enter no more into him.*
>
> *And the spirit cried, and rent him sore, and came out of him: and he was as one dead; insomuch that many said, He is dead.*

But Jesus took him by the hand, and lifted him up; and he arose (Mark 9:25-27).

Leaving an Open Door

Often people leave an open door for the enemy to come into their lives by their actions. They may not even realize they have done it. James 3:16 tells us strife can open the door for other evil spirits: *"For where envying and **strife** is, there is confusion and every evil work."*

If the enemy has come into your life or the life of someone you know, ask God to show you what opened the door. Then you can stop the enemy by simply closing that door. You close the door by repenting of your sin and asking the Lord to help you to stop.

For instance, if anger and strife are problems in your life, then losing your temper could be an open door to the devil. Use Philippians 4:13 to stop this from influencing you, *"I can do all things through Christ which strengthenth me."* After you have repented, asked the Lord to help you, and prayed the Scripture, if you still cannot conquer or control your anger, you need the Holy Spirit to tell you what to do. This principle may be better understood in an experience I had with my daughter.

Discernment From the Holy Spirit

When my daughter was in high school, she took a trip overseas with her German class. When she returned, she had nightmares in her room. Some of these nightmares were quite frightening to the point of seeing an apparition at the end of her bed. When she told me about it, I called my sister to come and pray with us. We went through her room and prayed. My sister has a strong gift of discerning of spirits. When she picked up the various items that my daughter had brought from Europe, she had a check in her spirit that one of them was cursed. When she touched that item, she had a burning sensation in her hand. There were many other souvenirs, but there was one certain item that she felt checked on. When we asked the Lord what to do, He told us to burn that item and then throw the remains away. We did so; afterward, the nightmares stopped, and my daughter could sleep in peace.

That souvenir was an open door for the enemy to harass my daughter. It gave the spirit a right to be there. Proverbs 26:2 shows how the enemy can come in: *"As the bird by wandering, as the swallow by flying, so the curse causeless shall not come."* A curse comes because of a reason—something causes it and gives it an open door. We used the gift of discerning of spirits to pinpoint what the open door was, and God gave us a Word of wisdom on how to close the door.

Before this incident, my sister and I had attended an Aglow retreat. The speaker had just returned from a mission trip in Europe. She told us of an incident where they had encountered a curse. One of the workers kept falling down. The team went to the Lord about it. After prayer they remembered there was a man who had volunteered with the mission's team for a short time and then left for England. This man had given all the women a necklace with a wooden cross on it. The lady who kept falling down had left her necklace on day and night. They realized those necklaces were cursed. They tried to burn the crosses, but they would not burn. The staff stood in a circle and put the necklaces in the middle and prayed in tongues. The crosses burned without being lighted!

Feeling and Knowing

The gift of discerning of spirits does not always work the same way, but the Holy Spirit will give you understanding each time. My spiritual daughter Barbara felt nauseated when she saw her next door neighbor. She knew in her spirit that the Lord was warning her. She lived in an apartment house at the time and avoided this man as best she could. He was later arrested for child molestation. The Holy Spirit made it known to Barbara to stay away from him.

Seeing and Knowing

Our friend Gwendolyn came to visit us and when she arrived I noticed that she was gray-looking in her face. The Holy Spirit spoke to me that a spirit of death was on her. My sister was there at the time and she saw the same look in Gwendolyn's face. We commanded the spirit of death off of her in Jesus' name. Her face immediately began to turn pink again and her appearance returned to normal. In this incident, we could see in Gwendolyn's face that something was wrong—that was the gift of discerning of spirits. We could see the spirit of death on Gwendolyn's face.

Not only are the Revelation Gifts valuable in praying through, but the Utterance Gifts are extremely important as well. Go on to the next chapter to find out more!

Remember these things:

- The gifts of the Spirit are for everyone to use. The Holy Spirit gives them to you as you need them.

- As a believer, you have authority over the devil and demons. You can bind them from influencing others in the name of Jesus.

- The word of wisdom tells you about a future event so you can take action and pray about it.

- The word of knowledge tells you about a current situation so you can take action and pray about it.

- Discerning of spirits tells you what spirits are influencing a situation or person so you can take authority over those spirits and bind them or cast them out.

Chapter 4

Vocal Gifts

Of the gifts listed in First Corinthians 12, the following three are considered the Vocal Gifts: the gift of speaking in tongues, the gift of interpretation of tongues, and prophecy. Each of these gifts involves giving a message from God to you or to others. You can find these gifts listed in First Corinthians 12:7-10:

> But the manifestation of the Spirit is given to every man to profit withal...to another prophecy...to another divers kinds of tongues; to another the interpretation of tongues.

The Vocal Gifts: Speaking in Tongues

Just before Jesus is taken up to Heaven, He tells the disciples not to leave town until they receive the power of the Holy Spirit. They stay in

Jerusalem ten days and pray. When the day of Pentecost has fully come they are all, 120 disciples, filled with the Holy Spirit and speak in other tongues as shown in Acts 2:4: *"And they were all filled with the Holy Ghost, and began to speak with other tongues, as the Spirit gave them utterance."*

The sign of speaking in tongues was the only one given throughout the Book of Acts as a sign that believers were filled with the Holy Spirit. Of course, you receive the Holy Spirit when you are born again—He is the one who bears you into God's Family, but the baptism of the Holy Spirit is a super amount of the Spirit that fills you to overflowing. Speaking in other tongues is the first (initial) sign of your infilling. There are many other signs that accompany this. Some people begin to understand the Bible better after they are filled with the Spirit. Some experience freedom in worship. After I received the baptism of the Holy Spirit, I was free to raise my hands in worship. I've even heard a number of people say that the trees and grass looked greener and the sunsets more vibrant. Acts 1:8 tells us that when the Holy Spirit comes upon you, you receive power:

> *But ye shall receive power, after that the Holy Ghost is come upon you: and ye shall be witnesses unto Me both in Jerusalem, and*

in all Judaea, and in Samaria, and unto the uttermost part of the earth (Acts 1:8).

Your Personal Gift

Speaking in other tongues is a personal gift that you use to build yourself up according to Jude 1:20: *"But ye, beloved, building up yourselves on your most holy faith, praying in the Holy Ghost."* It is also a way to pray when you don't know how to pray as mentioned in Romans 8:26:

Likewise the Spirit also helpeth our infirmities: for we know not what we should pray for as we ought: but the Spirit itself maketh intercession for us with groanings which cannot be uttered.

But God also has a gift of speaking in tongues which is a message in tongues from God.

The Gift of Speaking in Tongues

The gift of speaking in tongues referred to in First Corinthians 12:10 is intended to be used in a group setting for the purpose of helping everyone present. It is different than a personal prayer language which involves worshiping or praying God's will over a certain situation. This "gift" is a message directly from God intended for edification, exhortation, and comfort. The gift of speaking in tongues is intended to be spoken out loud so everyone can hear it and it must be interpreted in a language that can be understood by everyone. God also gives messages in common languages that do not require interpretation. This kind of message is called a "prophecy."

In First Corinthians 14, the apostle Paul gives us some important information about these gifts. Notice he first addresses the importance of prophecy over speaking in tongues without an interpretation. However, in the last paragraph he clarifies that it is appropriate to give a message in tongues if there is someone to interpret the message in a common language.

But he that prophesieth speaketh unto men to edification, and exhortation, and comfort.

He that speaketh in an unknown tongue edifieth himself; but he that prophesieth edifieth the church.

I would that ye all spake with tongues but rather that ye prophesied: for greater is he that prophesieth than he that speaketh with tongues, except he interpret, that the church may receive edifying (1 Corinthians 14:3-5).

Again, we read in this passage that the gift of prophecy is equal to the gift of speaking in tongues as long as it is used with the gift of interpretation of tongues. These vocal gifts edify believers. When they hear a message from God sent directly to them through this supernatural method, it encourages and builds their faith.

The Interpretation of Tongues

The gift of speaking in tongues is not just for a church meeting. It can be used in any setting where God wants to give a message to His children. Your own prayers in another tongue do not have to be interpreted, although they can be. But if a message in tongues is given in church, it needs to be interpreted. The apostle Paul tells us in First Corinthians 14:27-28, that in a group setting, it will not benefit the other believers unless there is someone to interpret:

If any man speak in an unknown tongue, let it be by two, or at the most by three, and that by course; and let one interpret. But if there be no

*interpreter, let him keep silence in the church;
and let him speak to himself, and to God*
(1 Corinthians 14:27-28).

There was a time in our church when no one
was able to give a message in tongues and an interpretation or a prophecy. I'd been around long
enough to know how valuable these gifts were to
the congregation. I determined in my heart to fast
and pray about receiving the gift of giving a message in tongues with the interpretation.

When my husband and I resigned as pastors of
our second church, we began attending my home
church. There were only two ladies in our church
who could interpret tongues. During that time,
God led me to give messages in tongues and one
of these ladies would interpret the message for the
church. Eventually both of the ladies moved away.
I could no longer give a message in tongues in
church without someone to interpret. Ten years
passed.

Kaye, my friend from Bible school, brought
her singing group to our church; she had the
gift of interpretation of tongues. Kaye and Wilbur laid hands on me and prayed I would receive
the gift of interpretation of tongues just as the
Scriptures say in Second Timothy 1:6. We are to
stir up the gift of God by the laying on of hands.

In Romans 1:11 Paul tells the Romans that he longed to see them so that he could impart to them a spiritual gift so that they would be established or grounded in God. In First Timothy 4:14 Paul tells Timothy not to neglect the gift that he received through prophecy when the elders laid hands on him.

I received the gift of interpretation of tongues that day. It began with just a verse coming up in my spirit. It was the verse, *"If My people shall... humble themselves, and pray..."* (2 Chron. 7:14). I had received verses like this in my spirit many times during those ten years, but I didn't recognize it was the Lord giving me a word for others. God would only give me the beginning of the verse— then as I stepped out in faith and spoke those words out, He would give me more until the interpretation was finished. An interpretation does not have to be an exact Scripture but it will line up with what the Word of God says. For me, it comes as a thought or phrase that I recognize is not my own.

I was so thrilled to be able to interpret and I used that gift often, but not everyone wanted to hear it. I learned that if the pastor did not make room in the service for it, then I had to be still. First Corinthians 14:32 says the spirit of the prophet is subject to the prophet. You are able to control the gifts that God gives you. For instance, you should not interrupt an altar call with a message in tongues or prophecy, because the Holy Spirit is moving people to receive salvation at that time.

Interpretation of Tongues Must Be Judged

The interpretation of tongues often comes in first person or third person. It is from the Lord but it comes through a human vessel, so it could be somewhat contaminated and must always be judged. It must agree with the Scripture, and listeners need to have the assurance that the message is from the Holy Spirit, Jesus the Son, or the Father.

I had assumed the messages were from Jesus, but one day in a ladies prayer group, the salutation was "My Daughters" and that would only be from our heavenly Father.

Our friend and prayer partner, Tory, operates in the gifts of the Spirit. When he gives a word from the Lord, sometimes it is from Jesus, sometimes from the Holy Spirit, and sometimes from the heavenly Father.

To Give Tongues and Interpretation

When the Lord prompts you to give a message in tongues, just start out speaking as the Lord leads you. Stop as soon as you feel prompted by the Lord to do so. It will probably be different than the usual prayer language that you use in your own prayer time.

To interpret your tongues, start at home by yourself. The Lord is always waiting to speak to you. He loves to fellowship and help His children. I keep a journal of messages that the Lord gives me in my own prayer time. I always date them; then I can read them later for encouragement. They too must be judged by God's Word and the inner witness of your spirit.

Prompted by the Lord

In a group setting, the Lord will prompt you to interpret. There will be a knowing in your spirit. It may be a Scripture as the Lord began with me or it may be a word of encouragement. Remember that these gifts are given for edification, exhortation, and comfort. Begin with what the Lord gives you. He usually does not give you the whole message, just a portion. As soon as you say that portion, another part will come. When the message is finished, you will not receive any more prompts from the Lord. Everyone who operates in this gift has to have a first time. Don't be discouraged if someone corrects you. It's by stepping out in faith that you learn how to operate in God's gifts.

Even if you are in a large church, you can start using your spiritual gifts in small groups. Then, as you begin to understand how to work with your gift, you can use it in larger groups.

The Gift of Prophecy

The gift of prophecy is like the interpretation of tongues without the tongues ahead of it. The first time I received the gift of prophecy was when I received the interpretation in my spirit before I could give the tongues. I was not used to that so it was frightening to me. Tongues always receive the attention of everyone. It's important, however, to follow God's leading. Do what He prompts you to do.

In First Corinthians 14, we learn that the gift of speaking in tongues is a sign to the unbeliever, and the interpretation or a prophecy is for the believer (verse 22) and the unbeliever (verse 25):

Wherefore tongues are for a sign, not to them that believe, but to them that believe not: but prophesying serveth not for them that believe not, but for them which believe.

If therefore the whole church be come together into one place, and all speak with tongues, and there come in those that are unlearned, or unbelievers, will they not say that ye are mad?

But if all prophesy, and there come in one that believeth not, or one unlearned, he is convinced of all, he is judged of all:

And thus are the secrets of his heart made manifest; and so falling down on his face he will worship God, and report that God is in you of a truth.

How is it then, brethren? when ye come together, every one of you hath a psalm, hath a doctrine, hath a tongue, hath a revelation, hath an interpretation. Let all things be done unto edifying (1 Corinthians 14:22-26).

Prophecy can be foretelling or forth-telling, telling of future events. John 16:13 tells us that the Holy Spirit will show us things to come and, of course, that would mean foretelling. Often however, prophecy is encouragement for current situations. Always use First Corinthians 14:3 to judge prophecy.

It must be for edification, exhortation, and comfort. In First Corinthians 14:5, Paul says he would rather that we prophesied because greater is he that prophesies than he that speaks with tongues, unless he interprets, because prophecy edifies everyone to understand what God is saying:

> But he that prophesieth speaketh unto men to edification, and exhortation, and comfort.
>
> He that speaketh in an unknown tongue edifieth himself; but he that prophesieth edifieth the church.
>
> I would that ye all spake with tongues but rather that ye prophesied: for greater is he that prophesieth than he that speaketh with tongues, except he interpret, that the church may receive edifying (1 Corinthians 14:3-5).

You can see how valuable the vocal gifts are in praying through, but there is one more set of gifts that is so important—the power gifts. Find out more in the next chapter!

Remember this:

- The vocal gifts are for edification, exhortation, and comfort in a group setting.

- The Lord will prompt you in your spirit if He has a message in tongues or prophecy for you to give.

- Only give a message in tongues if there is someone present to interpret. Otherwise, no one will understand.

- Everyone has a first time, so don't be discouraged if you are corrected.

Chapter 5

Power Gifts

The power gifts are spiritual gifts with amazing, supernatural results. They may seem impossible to the natural man or woman, but they are easy for God! These three gifts include: the gift of faith, gifts of healing, and working of miracles.

The Gift of Faith

When a super amount of faith rises up within you for a certain situation, it is called "the gift of faith." It is different than the kind of faith you have all the time. The Scriptures list faith as a fruit of the Spirit in Galatians 5. I call this "fruit faith." It is the kind of faith you have for every day.

But the fruit of the Spirit is love, joy, peace, longsuffering, gentleness, goodness, faith, meekness, temperance: against such there is no law (Galatians 5:22-23).

Fruit faith is the same as the faith that God gives to every man: *"...but to think soberly, according as God hath dealt to every man the measure of faith"* (Rom. 12:3). Fruit faith or "the measure of faith" is given by God to every person and is always with you. Fruit faith grows as you read the Bible and pray in tongues. We find this in Romans chapter 10 and the Book of Jude.

So then faith cometh by hearing, and hearing by the word of God (Romans 10:17).

But ye, beloved, building up yourselves on your most holy faith, praying in the Holy Ghost, keep yourselves in the love of God, looking for the mercy of our Lord Jesus Christ unto eternal life (Jude 1:20-21).

When you read the Word, apply it to your life, and it comes to pass; your faith grows.

You develop your "everyday" faith by working through the challenges of life that happen every day. In life experiences your faith in God allows the Lord to intervene for you. Those positive answers to faith inspire you to move out again in faith. That is how faith grows stronger. Like a muscle, the more you use it, the stronger it grows.

Just as reading the Bible causes your faith to grow according to Romans 10:17, hearing the Lord speak a Word directly to your spirit also causes your faith to grow. When a Word like this comes to pass, you begin to move from faith to faith and glory to glory. In Second Corinthians 3, the Scripture shows us that as we look into the Word of God—whether that be the written Word or the Lord speaking a Word to us—we are changed from glory to glory.

> *But we all, with open face beholding as in a glass the glory of the Lord, are changed into the same image from glory to glory, even as by the Spirit of the Lord* (2 Corinthians 3:18).

A Super Amount of Faith

The gift of faith is not the same as the measure of faith God gives to every person. It's a super amount of faith when you need it, but you don't have it all the time. We find reference to this in First Corinthians 12:7-9:

> *But the manifestation of the Spirit is given to every man to profit withal. For to one is given by the Spirit the word of wisdom; to another the word of knowledge by the same Spirit; to another faith by the same Spirit...*

The gift of faith works much like the other gifts of the Spirit. You have a knowing inside, a powerful knowing to believe in faith for circumstances to change. When praying through, this gift is important, especially when circumstances seem insurmountable.

After church one Sunday, Wilbur and I were invited to our friend Alta's house for dinner. After dinner she confided in me that she had just received a disturbing report from the doctor. The diagnosis was that she had a tumor. Immediately, I had a tremendous surge of faith for her healing. We prayed together that day. When Alta went back to the doctor the tumor had disappeared. She was healed. Faith just dropped into me for that situation. It was not the type of faith in my everyday life, but a super amount of faith.

There are many examples in Jesus' ministry when the gift of faith is working. In John 11 we read that Jesus raises Lazarus from the dead. Jesus uses the working of miracles for this situation, but He also operates in the gift of faith—a supernatural amount of faith that allows Him to bring someone back from the dead. The following account describes the miracle.

> *Jesus saith unto her, Said I not unto thee, that, if thou wouldest believe, thou shouldest*

see the glory of God? Then they took away the stone from the place where the dead was laid. And Jesus lifted up His eyes, and said, Father, I thank Thee that Thou hast heard Me. And I knew that Thou hearest Me always: but because of the people which stand by I said it, that they may believe that Thou hast sent Me. And when He thus had spoken, He cried with a loud voice, Lazarus, come forth. And he that was dead came forth, bound hand and foot with graveclothes: and his face was bound about with a napkin. Jesus saith unto them, Loose him, and let him go (John 11:40-44).

The Bible tells us in First Corinthians 13 of the gift of faith in respect to love. Without love, even amazing faith is worthless:

Though I speak with the tongues of men and of angels, but have not love, I have become sounding brass or a clanging cymbal. And though I have the gift of prophecy, and understand all mysteries and all knowledge, and though I have all faith, so that I could remove mountains, but have not love, I am nothing (1 Corinthians 13:1-2 NKJV).

At the end of Chapter 13, in verse 13, God shows us just how important faith is when He groups it together with hope and love: *"And now abide faith, hope, love, these three; but the greatest of these is love"* (1 Corinthians 13:13 NKJV).

Love is the most important and our foundation for anything we do in Christ, but faith is important too. When praying through, God gives this amazing gift that supersedes our natural mind and makes a way for miracles and healing to come into the earth.

The Gifts of Healing

The gifts of healing are specifically for the body— physical and emotional. When the gifts of healing are operating, they can manifest immediately in someone's body or they can manifest over a period of time. The gifts of healing are plural in the Bible because there are many different kinds and they come in different ways:

> *But the manifestation of the Spirit is given to every man to profit withal. For to one is given by the Spirit the word of wisdom; to another the word of knowledge by the same Spirit; To another faith by the same Spirit; to another the **gifts of healing** by the same Spirit* (1 Corinthians 12:7-9).

The gifts of the Spirit often work together, especially where the gifts of healing are concerned. Many times the three power gifts team up: the gifts of healing, the gift of faith, and the working of miracles. When someone's physical or emotional condition starts to improve after prayer, it is considered a healing. But if the healing is instant, it is a miracle of healing. There are many ways to receive healing, and you need to stay open to the Lord's leading in each case.

Types of Healing

The prayer of faith as taught in James 5:14-16 shows if we have the elders of the church lay hands on us and anoint with oil, that we can be healed.

> *Is any sick among you? let him call for the elders of the church; and let them pray over him, anointing him with oil in the name of the Lord: And the prayer of faith shall save the sick, and the Lord shall raise him up; and if he have committed sins, they shall be forgiven him* (James 5:14-15).

Laying hands on the sick as taught in Mark Chapter 16 also shows us another way.

And these signs shall follow them that believe; In My name shall they cast out devils; they shall speak with new tongues; They shall take up serpents; and if they drink any deadly thing, it shall not hurt them; they shall lay hands on the sick, and they shall recover (Mark 16:17-18).

Taking communion as taught in First Corinthians chapter 11 is another way to receive healing. The Lord's body was broken so we can be healed. When we honor Him by taking communion, we can release our faith for healing.

For I have received of the Lord that which also I delivered unto you, that the Lord Jesus the same night in which He was betrayed took bread: And when He had given thanks, He brake it, and said, Take, eat: this is My body, which is broken for you: this do in remembrance of Me (1 Corinthians 11:23-24).

First Peter 2:24 also shows us a Scripture that we can stand on in all situations of healing and even as a preventive way to build our faith to fight off sickness.

Who His own self bare our sins in His own body on the tree, that we, being dead to sins, should live unto righteousness: by whose stripes ye were healed (1 Peter 2:24).

Healing Actions

Sometimes the Holy Spirit reveals an action that will release His healing power. Believers should not try to do the same action the Lord told someone else to do, but listen in their inner being for specific directions from the Lord. In the Book of Second Kings, the Lord instructed Hezekiah to put a cake of figs on his boil and he would recover.

In those days Hezekiah became mortally ill. And Isaiah the prophet the son of Amoz came to him and said to him, "Thus says the LORD, 'Set your house in order, for you shall die and not live.'"

Then he turned his face to the wall and prayed to the LORD, saying,

"Remember now, O LORD, I beseech You, how I have walked before You in truth and with a whole heart and have done what is good in Your sight" And Hezekiah wept bitterly.

Before Isaiah had gone out of the middle court, the word of the LORD came to him, saying,

"Return and say to Hezekiah the leader of My people, 'Thus says the LORD, the God of your father David, "I have heard your prayer,

I have seen your tears; behold, I will heal you. On the third day you shall go up to the house of the LORD.

"I will add fifteen years to your life, and I will deliver you and this city from the hand of the king of Assyria; and I will defend this city for My own sake and for My servant David's sake."'"

Then Isaiah said, "Take a cake of figs." And they took and laid it on the boil, and he recovered (2 Kings 20:1-7 NASB).

Jesus demonstrated a unique action when He put mud on the blind man's eyes.

As long as I am in the world, I am the light of the world.

When He had thus spoken, He spat on the ground, and made clay of the spittle, and He anointed the eyes of the blind man with the clay, and said unto him, Go, wash in the pool of Siloam, (which is by interpretation, Sent.) He went His way therefore, and washed, and came seeing (John 9:5-7).

Some evangelists have the gift of healing and many are healed in their meetings. Hope rises when you see others healed, and the praise and worship creates an atmosphere that welcomes the Holy Spirit. People are encouraged in their faith to receive God's blessings.

Some are gifted to believe for backs to be healed or maybe cancer, and that's why the Bible says "gifts" of healing. God chooses to give the gifts to various people, but there is always a way to be healed. You have to seek God on how He wants to work with you.

The Working of Miracles

The working of miracles produces something. You can actually see a miracle. The working of miracles comes from praying and receiving a supernatural answer or from using your authority in Christ to command things to change. It could be supernatural provision, an instant healing, or restoration of someone's emotions. This gift is mentioned in First Corinthians 12:

> *To another the working of miracles; to another prophecy; to another discerning of spirits; to another divers kinds of tongues; to another the interpretation of tongues:*

But all these worketh that one and the selfsame
Spirit, dividing to every man severally as he
will (1 Corinthians 12:10-11).

The apostle Paul mentions the working of miracles again at the end of the chapter.

And God hath set some in the church, first
apostles,   secondarily   prophets,   thirdly
teachers, after that miracles, then gifts of
healings, helps, governments, diversities of
tongues. Are all apostles? are all prophets?
are all teachers? are all workers of miracles?
Have all the gifts of healing? do all speak with
tongues? do all interpret? But covet earnestly
the best gifts: and yet shew I unto you a more
excellent way (1 Corinthians 12:28-31).

Miracles in the Bible

Although First Corinthians does not give us a lot of teaching on how to operate in the working of miracles, the Bible is full of examples of miracles that we can learn from. The Gospels—Matthew, Mark, Luke, and John—are full of examples of miracles that Jesus performed. There are also a number of miracles in the Book of Acts. We are given an account of just one instance of those miracles in Acts chapter 8.

> *Then Philip went down to the city of Samaria, and preached Christ unto them. And the people with one accord gave heed unto those things which Philip spake, hearing and seeing the miracles which he did. For unclean spirits, crying with loud voice, came out of many that were possessed with them: and many taken with palsies, and that were lame, were healed. And there was great joy in that city* (Acts 8:5-8).

Miracles Today

I have experienced the gift of miracles several times in my life especially concerning the weather. Once while Wilbur and I and our oldest boy were traveling through Wyoming, we were caught in a blizzard. The temperature was far below zero; the wind was blowing snow, so it was almost impossible to see. Wilbur stopped to help pull someone out of the ditch. When our car cooled off so fast, we realized how quickly someone could freeze. I became fearful and our oldest son began to be frightened as well. Fear can be catchy, but so can faith. It came up in my spirit this was only wind and Jesus spoke to the wind and commanded it to be still. Since Jesus gave us His authority, I thought, "Well, I can do that too." I spoke to the wind and commanded it to be still. The wind stopped immediately! The sun came out. We had sunshine the rest of our trip that day.

Miracle Rain

As farmers, we were very dependent upon the weather. One very dry summer we were desperate for rain. The crops were going to dry up in the field if we did not get some quickly. Wilbur went outside and stood on the road that faces our land and began to pray for rain. That night, the rain came in— several inches we so desperately needed. The rain, however, only fell on our land and on our Christian neighbor's land. We were extremely thankful for the amazing miracle.

Financial Miracles

We've also had many financial miracles. Some were instant and some took time. Wilbur and I have always given tithes and offerings because we believe in laying up our treasure in Heaven (see Matt. 6:20). Even though circumstances were not always in our favor, especially living through some very tough years on the farm, I have to say God always found a way to take care of us. We never went without what we needed. Sometimes I would be discouraged because we weren't able to give as much as I would have liked, but God has always been faithful. He encourages us when we feel defeated and sends reminders to us that He is greater than any circumstance! If you are discouraged about your finances, find the Scriptures in the Bible that deal with finances and study them. Pray those Scriptures over your life and you will see your circumstances change. It might not be exactly the way you wanted, but God is always faithful.

One year Charles and Francis Hunter were speaking in a nearby city, and my back was healed in their meeting. They encouraged us to keep track of the offerings we gave at the meeting because they were going to pray a hundred-fold blessing over it. We gave fifty dollars that night, which at that time was quite a bit for us. Within one year, we received an unexpected $5,000 that we really needed. We did indeed receive a hundred-fold return.

Miracle Sale

In 1990 Wilbur and I were ready to retire from farming and needed to sell our farm. But my dad had instilled in me that I should never sell the land. Therefore, I was hesitant to sell. Wilbur asked me if the Lord brought someone to us who would offer to buy it out of the clear blue, would I then be willing to sell? We would not have to put the farm up for sale. We would just pray and wait. Wilbur had a certain dollar amount in mind; we agreed together that we would sell if the deal that Wilbur posed to me materialized. Now I thought, "Surely, no one would come and offer to buy our land; plus, the price that Wilbur has in mind is much higher than anyone would pay."

Three months later, sure enough, a man came down the driveway and offered to buy our farm. And he said, "Do you have a price in mind?"

Wilbur told him the price and he responded, "That doesn't sound too bad."

Needless to say, we sold the farm! God taught us a powerful lesson as we went through this experience. Some Scriptures to stand on for financial miracles are as follows: 2 Corinthians 8:9; 2 Corinthians 9:6-15; Matthew 9:29; Matthew 19:26; Matthew 21:22; Psalm 1:1-3; 3 John 2; and Philippians 4:19.

Other Gifts From God

The Bible mentions other gifts in the Scriptures including the five ministry gifts in Ephesians 4:11: apostles, prophets, evangelists, pastors, and teachers. There are also seven motivational gifts mentioned in Romans 12:6-8: prophecy, ministry, teaching, exhortation, giving, ruling, and mercy. Study of these gifts will help you understand your role in the Body of Christ, but the gifts of the Spirit that we have just reviewed are for everyone and available when needed. The Scripture admonishes us to desire spiritual gifts because we need them for ourselves and those in our circle of influence.

> But earnestly desire and zealously cultivate the greatest and best gifts and graces (the higher gifts and the choicest graces). And yet I will show you a still more excellent way [one that is better by far and the highest of them all—love] (1 Corinthians 12:31 AMP).

Follow the way of love and eagerly desire spiritual gifts, especially the gift of prophecy (1 Corinthians 14:1 NIV).

The Gifts of the Spirit Operate Together

The gifts of the Spirit blend together just like a rainbow. Sometimes you cannot tell the difference between one and the other because they flow together so beautifully. We can see an instance of this in Acts chapter 9. Saul who has been persecuting the Church receives a miracle transformation and becomes the apostle Paul.

And as he journeyed, he came near Damascus: and suddenly there shined round about him a light from heaven: And he fell to the earth, and heard a voice saying unto him, Saul, Saul, why persecutest thou me? And he said, Who art thou, Lord? And the Lord said, I am Jesus whom thou persecutest: it is hard for thee to kick against the pricks. And he trembling and astonished said, Lord, what wilt thou have me to do? And the Lord said unto him, Arise, and go into the city, and it shall be told thee what thou must do. And the men which journeyed with him stood speechless, hearing a voice, but seeing no man. And Saul arose from the earth; and when his eyes were opened, he saw no man: but they led him by the hand, and brought him into Damascus. And he was three days without sight, and neither did eat nor drink (Acts 9:3-9).

Paul had a vision from God and talked with Jesus. It was the way the Lord got Paul's attention. The Lord then found a disciple to help Saul. Notice in the next verses how the Lord spoke to Ananias and how He responded. The Lord spoke to him as his Lord, but also as his friend. God speaks to us the same way.

And there was a certain disciple at Damascus, named Ananias; and to him said the Lord in a vision, Ananias. And he said, Behold, I am here, Lord. And the Lord said unto him, Arise, and go into the street which is called Straight, and enquire in the house of Judas for one called Saul, of Tarsus: for, behold, he prayeth, and hath seen in a vision a man named Ananias coming in, and putting his hand on him, that he might receive his sight. Then Ananias answered, Lord, I have heard by many of this man, how much evil he hath done to Thy saints at Jerusalem: And here he hath authority from the chief priests to bind all that call on

Thy name. But the Lord said unto him, Go thy way: for he is a chosen vessel unto Me, to bear My name before the Gentiles, and kings, and the children of Israel: For I will shew him how great things he must suffer for My name's sake (Acts 9:10-16).

The Lord gave Ananias a word of knowledge so he would know about Saul. When the Lord told Ananias what to do, that was a word of wisdom. Ananias had to operate in the gift of faith for this situation, because in the natural, Saul had been a great enemy of the Christians and could have harmed Ananias.

And Ananias went his way, and entered into the house; and putting his hands on him said, Brother Saul, the Lord, even Jesus, that appeared unto thee in the way as thou camest, hath sent me, that thou mightest receive thy sight, and be filled with the Holy Ghost. And immediately there fell from his eyes as it had been scales: and he received sight forthwith, and arose, and was baptized. And when he had received meat, he was strengthened. Then was Saul certain days with the disciples which were at Damascus. And straightway he preached Christ in the synagogues, that He is the Son of God (Acts 9:17-20).

Ananias was operating in the working of miracles when he laid hands on Saul. Saul was instantly healed, filled with the Spirit, and began to preach the Gospel. It was a physical miracle and a spiritual miracle. As you learn to work with the Holy Spirit, the gifts can operate together or separately as the Holy Spirit directs just as He did with Ananias.

Counterfeit Gifts

For every good gift God has, satan has worked to produce a counterfeit. All gifts must be judged. The Holy Spirit lives in you and will lead you by the peace in your heart. Don't just accept a "word from the Lord" as Gospel without checking whether it lines up with Scripture and it bears witness in your own spirit.

But the anointing which you have received from Him abides in you, and you do not need that anyone teach you; but as the same anointing teaches you concerning all things, and is true, and is not a lie, and just as it has taught you, you will abide in Him (1 John 2:27 NKJV).

The Gifts of the Spirit Sandwich

In summary, the gifts of the Spirit are named in First Corinthians 12. We discover that they do not work without love in First Corinthians 13. We are instructed on how to use the gifts of the Spirit in First Corinthians chapter 14. I call this the gifts of the Spirit sandwich. All the gifts would just not taste very good without love.

- 1 Corinthians 12—Gifts (Bread)

- 1 Corinthians 13—Love (Meat)

- 1 Corinthians 14—Instructions (Bread)

There are so many ways the Holy Spirit works. I will try to cover some of them in chapters to come. In Hosea 4:6 we are told, *"My people are destroyed for lack of knowledge..."* As we learn more about the Holy Spirit, we are able to stand up against the enemy and avoid being destroyed. In the next chapter we will discover some important weapons the Lord has provided to battle against our enemy.

Remember this:

- The miracle gifts are for you to use when they are needed. The Lord will prompt you to use the gift of faith to believe for healing and miracles.

- It's important to follow God's lead when operating in these gifts. Only He knows exactly what to do for the miracle or healing to take place in the earth.

- The gift of faith is different from the measure of faith that every believer has. It is a supernatural amount of faith for a certain situation.

Chapter 6

Praying in Jesus' Name and by His Blood

Recently our prayer team got a burden for my son. We prayed a long time in English and in other tongues. We declared the Scriptures for protection over him—Psalm 91, Psalm 34:7, and Isaiah 58:8. The burden did not lift. We bound the enemy and cancelled his assignments against our son. We worshiped the Lord and gave thanksgiving, but we still felt burdened for him. Finally, Becky spoke up and said, "Let's pray about word curses."

The Holy Spirit led me then to break the word curses against him in the name of Jesus Christ. We also spoke Scriptures over him, including Isaiah 54:17. We did that together and the burden lifted. We prayed through!

I refer to these kinds of prayers as "warfare prayers." It's a powerful way for you, as a Christian, to combat the attacks of satan. It can be a lot of hard work, but it's also an amazing adventure that helps people so much. The rewards are worth it. There are a number of spiritual weapons God has given us to use in prayer. These weapons are valuable in our own prayer lives and when praying for others. Second Corinthians 10 shows us the battle that we are to fight. It's not against people, but against spiritual enemies. Much of this warfare is in our minds—a battle of thoughts. Satan's strategy against the human race is to defeat them in their minds:

> For though we walk in the flesh, we do not war after the flesh: (For the weapons of our warfare are not carnal, but mighty through God to the pulling down of strong holds;) Casting down imaginations, and every high thing that exalteth itself against the knowledge of God, and bringing into captivity every thought to the obedience of Christ (2 Corinthians 10:3-5).

As believers, we fight negative thoughts perpetrated by satan or his demonic force in our individual lives. Negative thoughts may include feeling defeat, worry, fear, depression, anger, and many other negative emotions. On a larger scale, these negative thoughts, left unchecked, become philosophies by which entire people groups live. They can be perverted to the point of great evil. An example may be terrorists who murder and torture innocent people. The spiritual weapons God has given us can win against these negative thoughts and bring victory in our own life and in the lives of others.

The Name of Jesus

In the first chapter, I mentioned briefly the importance of praying in the name of Jesus. His name is powerful and when we speak His name in faith, things change. Jesus became our mediator to God when He died as an innocent man, a man without sin and shed His blood for our sins: *"For there is one God, and one mediator between God and men, the man Christ Jesus"* (1 Tim. 2:5).

John 14 tells us Jesus instructs His disciples to ask the Father anything in His name and their requests would be answered. *"And whatsoever ye shall ask in **my name**, that will I do, that the Father may be glorified in the Son. If ye shall ask any thing in **my name**, I will do it"* (John 14:13-14). That is a very powerful statement made by Jesus Himself. Anything we ask in His name, He will do.

In the Book of Acts, Peter and John are on their way to the temple when they notice a lame man. They speak to the man to look at them. Notice how Peter and John pray:

*And he gave heed unto them, expecting to receive something of them. Then Peter said, Silver and gold have I none; but such as I have give I thee: In the **name of Jesus Christ of Nazareth** rise up and walk. And he took him by the right hand, and lifted him up: and immediately his feet and ankle bones received strength. And he leaping up stood, and walked, and entered with them into the temple, walking, and leaping, and praising God (Acts 3:5-8).*

Healing came to the man at the temple gate through the name of Jesus. His name carries authority that exceeds natural law. Later Peter and John are arrested for healing the lame man. When Peter is put before the elders, he defends himself and the name of Jesus Christ. There is power in that name.

*Be it known unto you all, and to all the people of Israel, that by the **name of Jesus Christ of Nazareth**, whom ye crucified, whom God raised from the dead, even by Him doth this man stand here before you whole. This is the stone which was set at nought of you builders, which is become the head of the corner. Neither is there salvation in any other: for there is none other name under heaven given among men, whereby we must be saved (Acts 4:10-12).*

We receive salvation and every other good thing from the Father through Jesus. In prayer, it is vital that we pray in the name of Jesus. Since there are people who have been named "Jesus" by their families, I often pray in the name of "Jesus Christ" or "Jesus Christ of Nazareth." The definition of *Christ* is "the Messiah" or "the Anointed One."[1]

The Blood of Jesus

There is power in the blood of Jesus. In praying through I always plead the blood of Jesus over myself and my family. Just as in a court of law where you may plead, "not guilty," you can plead the blood of Jesus for your protection, healing, and deliverance.

In the Old Testament when Moses is trying to free the Hebrews from the Egyptians, the final plague God pronounces upon them is that their firstborn would die. The Hebrews escape the plague when they put the blood of the sacrificial lamb on their doorposts and the lintels of their homes to protect them from the death angel. That incident is the first Passover. The plague passes over the house where the blood is found. This act is a symbol of Jesus' blood, the all-inclusive redemption from sin and protection from evil.

Then Moses called for all the elders of Israel, and said unto them, Draw out and take you a lamb according to your families, and kill the passover.

And ye shall take a bunch of hyssop, and dip it in the blood that is in the bason, and strike the lintel and the two side posts with the blood that is in the bason; and none of you shall go out at the door of his house until the morning.

For the LORD will pass through to smite the Egyptians; and when He seeth the blood upon the lintel, and on the two side posts, the LORD will pass over the door, and will not suffer the destroyer to come in unto your houses to smite you.

And ye shall observe this thing for an ordinance to thee and to thy sons for ever.

And it shall come to pass, when ye be come to the land which the LORD will give you, according as He hath promised, that ye shall keep this service.

And it shall come to pass, when your children shall say unto you, What mean ye by this service?

That ye shall say, It is the sacrifice of the LORD's passover, who passed over the houses of the children of Israel in Egypt, when He smote the Egyptians, and delivered our houses. And the people bowed the head and worshipped (Exodus 12:21-27).

As New Testament believers, we have received the blood of Jesus that has the power to redeem us from sin. When we put faith in Jesus' blood shed for our sins, we receive forgiveness and protection:

And from Jesus Christ, who is the faithful witness, and the first begotten of the dead, and the prince of the kings of the earth. Unto Him that loved us, and washed us from our sins in His own blood (Revelation 1:5).

Not only are our sins remitted when we receive Jesus as Lord, we constantly have the blood of Jesus Christ to keep us free from bondage of sin. His blood still speaks for us. *"But if we walk in the light, as He is in the light, we have fellowship one with another, and the blood of Jesus Christ His Son cleanseth us from all sin"* (1 John 1:7). The enemy cannot cross the blood line of Jesus. Just as the death angel could not cross the blood in the Old Testament, so much more does Jesus' precious blood protect us today.

The Power of the Blood

In years past, Wilbur belonged to a Gospel businessmen's group heading up a chapter in our home town. We were friends with a gentleman who was one of the representatives from Minnesota. He told several stories that clarify the need of pleading the blood, especially around your property.

Before serving the true and living God, he had been involved in satan worship. After he was born again, there were several witches that were angry about this change and they sent out curses on him. He said he did not dare lose his temper even in traffic because he did not want any sin in his life. Sin could be an open door for those curses to stick to him. One witch brought a can of kerosene to his house to burn the house down. He had prayed the blood of Jesus around his property. When the witch reached his property line, she ran into an invisible shield. She dropped the can of kerosene and ran!

On another occasion, a rock with a curse tied to it was thrown at his picture window. The rock hit an invisible shield and dropped to the ground. The rock dropped right where he had prayed for the blood line of Jesus to surround his property. First Peter 1 tells us because of the precious blood of Christ, our faith and hope are in God. One of the privileges and rights He gave us is to plead and declare His blood over our lives, our property, and our bodies for our protection:

> *For you know that God paid a ransom to save you from the empty life you inherited from your ancestors. And the ransom He paid was not mere gold or silver. It was the precious blood of Christ, the sinless, spotless Lamb of God. God chose Him as your ransom long before the world began, but He has now revealed Him to you in these last days.*
>
> *Through Christ you have come to trust in God. And you have placed your faith and hope in God because He raised Christ from the dead and gave Him great glory* (1 Peter 1:18-21 NLT).

You Can Plead the Blood

I plead the blood of Jesus Christ over myself and my family every day. My faith in His precious blood is released every day for our protection, our healing, and our provision. When I am praying for other people, I always plead the blood of Jesus over myself and my own family first because it secures a supernatural barrier of protection from the attacks of the enemy. You might pray it this way, "I plead the blood of Jesus over (your name), (your family), my home, and my property. Thank you, Father God that no evil can cross the blood of Jesus."

When you stay in a strange place or in a motel, you may not realize what evil spirits could be lingering there. You do not know what happened in that room before you came or who occupied it, but you can plead the blood of Jesus over that room for your protection. The blood of Jesus will cleanse the room from any evil curses or spirits. Sometimes I declare the room to be washed in the blood of Jesus Christ. I also wash the air above and the earth beneath. We find in Ephesians 2:2 that satan is considered the *"prince of the power of the air"* and in Ephesians 4:8 Jesus descended to the lower parts of the earth to defeat satan, but we have his authority to enforce satan's defeat here on the earth. I often cleanse the air above and the earth beneath to make sure I've got everything covered.

I want to reiterate how important it is to use the name of *Jesus Christ of Nazareth* and plead the blood of *Jesus Christ of Nazareth* when praying warfare prayers. It is only in Christ that we have authority in spiritual matters. Remember this:

- There is power in the name of Jesus and it is through His name that we are given authority over the power of darkness and the things of this world. Always pray "in the name of Jesus Christ."

- The shed blood of Jesus cleanses us from sin and gives us the right to walk in His authority. You can "plead" or "declare" the blood of Jesus Christ for protection, healing, and provision.

Endnote

1. Online Etymology Dictionary, s.v. *Christ*, http://www.etymonline.com/index.php?term=Christ; accessed 7/26/2010.

Chapter 7

The Power of Words

Early in my married life I began to watch soap operas. I was hooked on those shows and felt convicted. I was constantly under condemnation about it and in my desperation I began to quote First John 1:9: *"If we confess our sins, He is faithful and just to forgive us our sins, and to cleanse us from all unrighteousness."* I would say it out loud many times. As I said the Word, my desires began to change and I started to despise those shows. Soon I was not watching them at all. The Word is so powerful when you speak it out over your life and the lives of others. God wants us to stay free from sin and deception and He has given us powerful weapons to use, but we must take action for these weapons to be effective.

Speaking the Promises of God

The same way you receive salvation is how you receive everything from the Lord; you believe in your heart and declare it to be true with your words. Romans 10:9-10 shows this principle:

> *That if you confess with your mouth the Lord Jesus and believe in your heart that God has raised Him from the dead, you will be saved. For with the heart one believes unto righteousness, and with the mouth confession is made unto salvation* (Romans 10:9-10 NKJV).

The Word of the Lord came to the children of Israel in Isaiah chapter 1. The Lord invited the Hebrews to come and talk to Him. When they did, their sins would be cleansed. It wasn't their sacrifices He desired, because they were already doing that. It was their heart. When they came to talk with Him is when He said their sins would be cleansed. *"I, the LORD, invite you to come and talk it over. Your sins are scarlet red, but they will be whiter than snow or wool"* (Isaiah 1:18 CEV). It's not only what you say to God, but your heart's motives that count. And that principle is true when you do anything for the Lord—especially in praying through.

The Lord and His Word are one and they are eternal. In Matthew 24:35 Jesus said it this way, *"Heaven and earth shall pass away, but My words shall not pass away."* As you begin to put His Word down in your heart, it will cause you to overcome.

Jesus tells the disciples how important it is to know His Word: *"If ye abide in Me, and My words abide in you, ye shall ask what ye will, and it shall be done unto you"* (John 15:7).

We know that when we speak the promises that are found in the Word of God that we are speaking in line with God's will. God's Word for us is His will for us. It directs us and guides us in all the decisions of life. Even in the Old Testament we find how important God's Word is to our success: *"Thy word is a lamp unto my feet, and a light unto my path"* (Ps. 119:105). In the next verses the writer of the Psalm shows us that he says God's Word and does it: *"I have sworn, and I will perform it, that I will keep Thy righteous judgments"* (Ps. 119:106).

In Isaiah 55 the Lord was speaking about His everlasting covenant. This Scripture tells us how powerful the Word of the Lord is. It *will* come to pass. When we agree in faith with what God says about us in His Word, our lives begin to change and prosper just as this verse reads:

> *So shall My word be that goes forth from My mouth; It shall not return to Me void, but it shall accomplish what I please, and it shall prosper **in the thing** for which I sent it* (Isaiah 55:11 NKJV).

The apostle Paul tells us in Second Corinthians how important it is to believe in our hearts and to speak it out loud in respect to exercising our faith: *"We having the same spirit of faith, according as it is written, I believed, and therefore have I spoken; we also believe, and therefore speak"* (2 Cor. 4:13).

When you are faced with a difficult situation, find Scriptures that can back you up. There are many promises in the Word of God that are given to you by God to help you. Stand on those Scriptures and speak them out loud over the trouble you are dealing with. You may even want to get a Bible promise book where God's promises are listed by topic. Then find those Scriptures in your Bible and outline them. Read them in context so you understand completely the promise of God. Then declare those promises as yours and begin to speak them over your life. Let God's Word work for you—He gave you those promises because you need them.

The Weapon of Breaking Word Curses

Our words are powerful, positive, and negative. People who curse other people can actually have an effect on them. Parents who speak negative words over their children can damage their children's future. Husbands and wives who speak negative things about their spouse can affect their relationships in terrible ways. In the Book of James, we realize how important it is to watch what we say. In chapter 3, verse 2 we find that the perfect man is the man who does not offend in his word. Starting in verse 6 we see how much damage a tongue can do:

> *And the tongue is a fire, a world of iniquity: so is the tongue among our members, that it defileth the whole body, and setteth on fire the course of nature; and it is set on fire of hell. For every kind of beasts, and of birds, and of serpents, and of things in the sea, is tamed, and hath been tamed of mankind: But the tongue can no man tame; it is an unruly evil, full of deadly poison. Therewith bless we God, even the Father; and therewith curse we men, which are made after the similitude of God. Out of the same mouth proceedeth blessing and cursing. My brethren, these things ought not so to be* (James 3:6-10).

We have to keep a check on ourselves that we do not curse others in frustration or anger. It is easy to fall into the trap of cursing those in authority— your boss, your pastor, even world leaders. Instead, bring these people up to the Lord in prayer and ask God to give them wisdom. The writer of Ecclesiastes warns us about this:

Curse not the king, no not in thy thought; and curse not the rich in thy bedchamber: for a bird of the air shall carry the voice, and that which hath wings shall tell the matter (Ecclesiastes 10:20).

Curses can come from angry people and curses can also come from people who dabble in the occult. Witches practice cursing others, sometimes for a fee or for their own diabolical reasons. All word curses can be broken by using the name of Jesus and by pleading the blood of Jesus Christ. Isaiah 54:17 is an important verse to quote when breaking word curses or when anyone comes against you. It's a powerful promise from God that we can stand on.

No weapon that is formed against thee shall prosper; and every tongue that shall rise against thee in judgment Thou shalt condemn. This is the heritage of the servants of the LORD, and their righteousness is of Me, saith the LORD (Isaiah 54:17).

When our friend Brian was in college, he overheard two students experimenting by putting curses on two other students. One of the cursed students then left school and the other one got very, very sick. We know that sort of thing is real and especially when seasoned witches put spells or curses on people. But the blood of Jesus Christ can break those curses.

Psalm 37:12-18 gives a warning for the wicked who curse the righteous. It says they are in danger of the curse going into their own heart. Several years ago I heard a man tell a story about a coven of witches who had cursed a Spirit-filled man. They were out in the woods walking around an altar chanting a curse of heart attack on this man. Their priest held a knife up and stabbed a bird laid on an altar for a sacrifice. The warlock priest dropped dead of a heart attack at that very moment.

The Importance of Words

Watching our words is so important and we need to think about what we say when we pray. I found this out first hand when we were visiting some business owners and friends of ours on the West Coast. They owned a sporting store, but it was not in the best location and sales were slow. We prayed with them over the store and said, "Lord, get those clothes out of here!" Not long after that a pickup rammed the front window and all the clothes were stolen! It was a mess, but the insurance covered it. We learned an important lesson that we need to be led by the Spirit of God about what we say in our prayers. Proverbs 18:21 tells us: *"Death and life are in the power of the tongue, and those who love it will eat its fruit"* (NKJV). Pay attention to what you are saying and make sure your words are bringing life and not death.

Inner Vows

Inner vows are when someone makes a personal declaration to themselves. These personal covenants can be done so thoughtlessly people do not even realize they have done it. They may forget about what they have told themselves, but those vows can have a lasting effect on their life. The Word of God is clear that we are not to swear or vow, not even to ourselves:

> *But above all things, my brethren, swear not, neither by heaven, neither by the earth, neither by any other oath: but let your yea be yea; and your nay, nay; lest ye fall into condemnation* (James 5:12).

In Matthew 5:34, Jesus Himself warns us against making vows: *"But I say unto you, Swear not at all; neither by heaven; for it is God's throne."* In the New Living Translation this verse is even clearer: *"But I say, do not make any vows! Do not say, 'By heaven!'* [it is a sacred vow] *because heaven is God's throne."*

In John Loren Sanford's book, *Elijah Among Us,*[1] he tells of an incident of a girl who miscarried several times. The Lord showed her counselor that the girl had made an inner vow when she was young. She said to herself that she would never have a baby boy because her brothers had teased her and been mean to her. When she nullified or broke the vow verbally, she was able to have children.

We often hear the Scriptures Mark 11:23-24 in reference to receiving good things from God, but the opposite also works. If you say negative things about your life and believe them, then that is what you will receive.

For verily I say unto you, That whosoever shall say unto this mountain, Be thou removed, and be thou cast into the sea; and shall not doubt in his heart, but shall believe that those things which he saith shall come to pass; he shall have whatsoever he saith.

Therefore I say unto you, What things soever ye desire, when ye pray, believe that ye receive them, and ye shall have them (Mark 11:23-24).

Watch that you are not putting yourself down with negative words. The enemy can act on the negative words because you have declared them and your words have authority in the earth. Wars between families and even nations have been started by words. Train yourself to speak words of faith about yourself and your family. Negative words are powerful, but so are positive ones.

Generational Curses

Generational curses are inherited weaknesses that come down family blood lines. A generational curse could be a disease like diabetes or cancer, compulsive addictions like alcoholism or gambling, challenges with anger, and many other things. In the Book of Exodus, we find that the sins of the parents go down three or four generations. These sins or iniquities can become generational curses. In the same way, the blessings of the Lord go for a thousand generations.

You shall not bow down yourself to them or serve them; for I the Lord your God am a jealous God, visiting the iniquity of the fathers upon the children to the third and fourth generation of those who hate Me, But showing mercy and steadfast love to a thousand generations of those who love Me and keep My commandments (Exodus 20:5-6 AMP).

This curse was given in the Old Testament under the law given to the children of Israel under Moses, but Jesus redeemed us from the curse in the New Testament. We are no longer subject to generational curses and can be free from them by breaking them in the name of Jesus Christ.

Christ has redeemed us from the curse of the law, having become a curse for us (for it is written, 'Cursed is everyone who hangs on a tree'), that the blessing of Abraham might come upon the Gentiles in Christ Jesus, that we might receive the promise of the Spirit through faith (Galatians 3:13-14 NKJV).

When you cleanse your bloodline, you need to ask the Lord to wash it in the blood of Jesus Christ of Nazareth. You break generational curses in the name of Jesus Christ and with the blood of Jesus. Ask the Lord to wash the bloodline back ten generations on both sides of the family and from their bloodline to their children. For more information on this topic, Marilyn Hickey has an excellent book called *Breaking Generational Curses.*[2]

Remember this:

- The way you receive salvation is the same way you receive everything from God: by saying and believing (see Rom. 10:8-10).

- Words are important and can determine your destiny. Make sure you are saying what God's Word says about you and your life.

- Negative words can work against you when spoken by you or by others. You can take authority over those words and break their power in the name of Jesus Christ.

Endnotes

1. John Loren Sanford, *Elijah Among Us* (Ada, MI: Chosen Books, 2002).

2. Marilyn Hickey, *Breaking Generational Curses* (Tulsa, OK: Harrison House, 2000).

Chapter 8

Spiritual Weapons in Prayer

All the different tactics used in prayer may seem overwhelming, but when you are lead by the Holy Spirit, He will show you what to do. He works with you where you are and will bring to remembrance what you need. Having knowledge of these methods helps you to clearly understand His direction and builds faith in their effectiveness. The Word tells us: *"Study to shew thyself approved unto God, a workman that needeth not to be ashamed, rightly dividing the word of truth"* (2 Tim. 2:15).

Praying in Tongues

One of the strongest spiritual weapons we have is praying in tongues, as I have mentioned earlier. Remember, often you don't know what to pray, but when you yield yourselves to the Holy Spirit in prayer, He can pray the perfect prayer through you when you pray in tongues. Romans 8:26-28 shows us when we pray in the Spirit, the Holy Spirit works with Jesus and the Father God to pray the perfect prayer about that situation. When I do not know what to do about a situation, I pray in tongues for a while and then the Lord will show me the next step, usually by a knowing in my spirit.

Pulling Down Strongholds

The word *stronghold* in the phrase "pulling down strongholds" refers to a controlling evil spirit that has set up a pattern of negative thoughts in a person's mind, in a group of people, or even over a location. The Bible refers to strongholds in Second Corinthians 10:4: *"For the weapons of our warfare are not carnal, but mighty through God to the pulling down of strong holds."*

In Ephesians 6:12, the Scriptures tell us that our battle is not against people but against spiritual strongholds:

For we do not wrestle against flesh and blood, but against principalities, against powers, against the rulers of the darkness of this age, against spiritual hosts of wickedness in the heavenly places (Ephesians 6:12 NKJV).

The first time I heard about pulling down strongholds was at a women's retreat. The leadership warned us not to try it by ourselves, but to wait until we had enough of a group to be effective. The Holy Spirit will lead you about how many people you need for each situation. The speaker told a story of a pastor who tried it alone and was burned all over his body for no apparent natural reason. He had to be hospitalized and treated for six months.

God has not given us a spirit of fear or timidity in these situations, but He did give us common sense. Don't take on more than you can handle. Always rely on the leading of the Holy Spirit. In Second Timothy 1:7, the Scriptures show us that God has given us a sound mind and that we are not to be afraid of satan or his powers: *"For God hath not given us the spirit of fear; but of power, and of love, and of a sound mind."* This means that with God's help, we can overcome any attack of the enemy, but we need to consider carefully what we are doing and listen to the leading of the Holy Spirit. The Amplified version of the Bible translates a sound mind as follows: *"...of calm and well-balanced mind and discipline and self-control"* (2 Tim. 1:7).

Several months later, our pastor and about 25 other people were praying for our city and the Lord instructed us to pray against the strongholds in our town. Pulling down strongholds is a weapon that the Lord can use to bring freedom to an area, people group, or a person that has been oppressed by evil spirits. The Bible gives us the authority to pull down strongholds in Jesus' name, and He has given us the gifts of the Holy Spirit to help us.

The gift of discerning of spirits is very helpful in situations like this because it helps pinpoint what spirits are at work, and then you can pull them down. You cannot pull down the strongholds over the whole world; it is too big for you, but you can pull down the things concerning you, your family, or your church. Ask the Holy Spirit to show you what the strongholds are and then follow His leading.

It is so important to use Jesus' name in pulling down strongholds because His name is exalted above every other name. Every person, every angelic being, every demon, and satan himself will someday bow their knees to Jesus Christ.

Wherefore God also hath highly exalted Him, and given Him a name which is above every name:

That at the name of Jesus every knee should bow, of things in heaven, and things in earth, and things under the earth;

And that every tongue should confess that Jesus Christ is Lord, to the glory of God the Father (Philippians 2:9-11).

Binding and Loosing

The enemy comes against every person in one way or another, and the Word of God gives us authority to bind or break satan's assignments against us. We are also given authority to loose good things into the earth that counteract these attacks. Note what Jesus tells the disciples in the Book of Matthew:

Verily I say unto you, Whatsoever ye shall bind on earth shall be bound in heaven: and whatsoever ye shall loose on earth shall be loosed in heaven.

Again I say unto you, That if two of you shall agree on earth as touching any thing that they shall ask, it shall be done for them of My Father which is in heaven (Matthew 18:18-19).

In the New Living Translation, this verse sheds more light on how much authority God has given us as His children. What you prohibit and what you allow on earth is backed up by God with His authority from Heaven.

I tell you the truth, whatever you forbid on earth will be forbidden in heaven, and whatever you permit on earth will be permitted in heaven.

I also tell you this: If two of you agree here on earth concerning anything you ask, my Father in heaven will do it for you (Matthew 18:18-19 NLT).

Satan's assignments or attacks against you may be sickness, financial challenges, depression, fear, and a host of other things. When you realize you are under attack, take authority over those assignments and break them in the name of Jesus Christ.

Wrong attitudes in people and even yourself can often be the results of an attack of the enemy. You can bind those attitudes and negative thought patterns in the name of Jesus Christ. When you take authority and bind a bad attitude, that person can be freed up enough to realize that what they are thinking is incorrect. They are then free to make a decision to change. If they prohibit that attitude in their own life, they can stay free. Romans 12:2 admonishes us to be transformed by renewing our minds to what God's Word says. When people begin to renew their minds by reading and studying the Word of God, that Word replaces those negative attitudes with the truth that can keep them free.

My friend Becky asked the Lord to be loosed from the spirit of judgmental criticism. She was terribly critical of overweight people and every time she criticized someone, she gained weight. After prayer, instead of judging the people, she now prays for them and her weight is in check! In the following verse, Jesus lets us know that if we judge others, the same judgment will be used on us: *"Judge not, that you be not judged. For with what judgment you judge, you will be judged; and with the measure you use, it will be measured back to you"* (Matthew 7:1-2 NKJV).

Praise and Worship as a Weapon

Psalm 22:3 tells us the Lord inhabits the praises of His people. Evil spirits cannot stand to be in the presence of God. When you begin to worship and praise God, something happens in the spiritual realm that brings freedom and joy. In the Old Testament, many times when the people would worship and praise God, His glory would fill the temple as a cloud of smoke. Chronicles records the following incident:

> *When Solomon finished praying, fire came down from heaven and consumed the burnt*

*offering and the sacrifices, and the glory of the
LORD filled the temple. The priests could not
enter the temple of the LORD because the glory
of the LORD filled it. When all the Israelites
saw the fire coming down and the glory of
the LORD above the temple, they knelt on the
pavement with their faces to the ground, and
they worshiped and gave thanks to the LORD,
saying, "He is good; His love endures forever"*
(2 Chronicles 7:1-3 NIV).

Often when I am in my personal prayer time
or in a group, I feel led to stop and worship and
praise the Lord. Psalm 100:4 tells us to enter into
God's presence with thanksgiving and praise: *"Enter into His gates with thanksgiving, and into His
courts with praise: be thankful unto Him, and bless
His name."* The Book of Philippians instructs us
in prayer to be thankful before we bring our requests: *"Be careful for nothing; but in every thing
by prayer and supplication with thanksgiving let
your requests be made known unto God"* (Phil. 4:6).
In Psalm 92:1 we find it is a good thing to thank
the Lord and praise Him: *"It is a good thing to give
thanks unto the Lord, and to sing praises unto Thy
name, O most high."* There are many other places
in the Bible where there is record of praise and
thanksgiving. Make sure to remember this as part
of your prayer time.

Asking for the Lord to Send Angels

Are not all angels ministering spirits sent to serve those who will inherit salvation? (Hebrews 1:14 NIV)

Angels are ministers to the heirs of salvation. If you have accepted Jesus Christ as your Lord then you are an heir of salvation. God had sent angels to help you while you are here on the earth. There is much to be said on the topic of angels but in respect to praying through you need to know that you can request angelic assistance. Psalm 103:20 tells us that angels listen to God's Word or what lines up with God's Word. When we pray Scriptures over situations, we can be assured that angels will act according to what we pray: *"Bless the LORD, ye His angels, that excel in strength, that do His commandments, hearkening unto the voice of His word"* (Ps. 103:20).

For example if someone is in danger, you can pray Psalm 91:11 for that person. Just substitute the person's name that is in trouble and declare the angels of God have charge over them to keep them in all their ways: *"For He shall give His angels charge over thee, to keep thee in all thy ways"* (Ps. 91:11).

In the same way, you can hinder your angels from helping if your words do not line up with God's Word. They are listening for the words that follow the Scriptures. When I was just a little girl, a man came to start the first Pentecostal Church in our area. He came with his family in the month of March in a Model-T Ford with leather sidecurtains. About ten miles from our little town they got stuck in the snow. Pastor George cried to the Lord, "What shall I do?" Just then a handsome man with a team of horses pulled up and offered to pull them out. After they were out of deep snow, Pastor George turned to thank him, but he had disappeared! Psalm 91 was definitely working for Pastor George that day.

Psalm 34:7 is another Scripture to pray for angelic assistance: *The angel of the LORD encamps all around those who fear Him, and delivers them* (Ps. 34:7 NKJV).

Once when my friend Becky had back surgery one of the nurses was extremely unkind to her. Then later a very sweet nurse came into her room and stayed all afternoon. This nurse was able to turn Becky over in her bed by herself and it never caused her any pain. After the nurse left, Becky asked about her and no one knew who she was or where she came from. Angels are real here in the earth to help us. Don't hesitate to ask for angelic assistance if you need it.

Power of Agreement

In prayer, the act of agreeing with another believer makes an amazing difference. In Matthew 18:19 Jesus shows this principle: *"Again I say to you that if two of you agree on earth concerning anything that they ask, it will be done for them by My Father in heaven"* (Matt. 18:19 NKJV).

You have to agree in prayer—not disagree. Common sense tells you the prayer of agreement is answered when you agree with someone. Make sure you and your spouse or prayer partner are in unity. It's unity that brings results. When the pastors in a city pray together, things in their city can change. Unity in business also brings amazingly positive results. The Psalms reveal this truth:

> *How good and pleasant it is when brothers live together in unity! It is like precious oil poured on the head, running down on the beard, running down on Aaron's beard, down upon the collar of his robes. It is as if the dew of Hermon were falling on Mount Zion. For*

*there the LORD bestows His blessing, even
life forevermore* (Psalm 133:1-3 NIV).

There is a special bond when a husband and
wife agree for their children. The Bible says that
when a man and wife are joined in marriage they
become one flesh. Their agreement is a powerful
alliance against the enemy when praying for their
family. When our children were in high school
and college, Wilbur and I would hold hands and
agree. Sometimes we would have to stand in faith
for a while, but the answer would always come.
We prayed about our children's future spouses,
problems at school, relationships, jobs, and many
other things. In First Peter 3 we find that a man's
prayers can be hindered if he is mad at his wife!
(Keep in mind that the six verses preceding this
verse are about a wife being in submission to her
husband.)

> *Husbands, likewise, dwell with them with
> understanding, giving honor to the wife, as to
> the weaker vessel, and as being heirs together
> of the grace of life, that your prayers may not
> be hindered* (1 Peter 3:7 NKJV).

My friend Donna and I have prayed many times
for our children using the prayer of agreement. Her
children were about the same age as my children. It
was powerful and certainly helped get the children

through school safely. If you are struggling with a situation, find a believer to agree in prayer with you. You can even call the prayer lines of various ministries and find other believers to pray with you. Don't try to be an island to yourself; pray in agreement with other believers.

The Armor of God

In Ephesians 6, the apostle Paul gives us instructions on how to stand against the deception of satan and his demonic forces. Paul makes it clear that we are fighting a spiritual enemy and that by putting on our spiritual armor we can live in victory.

Finally, my brethren, be strong in the Lord and in the power of His might. Put on the whole armor of God, that you may be able to stand against the wiles of the devil. For we do not wrestle against flesh and blood, but against principalities, against powers, against the rulers of the darkness of this age, against spiritual hosts of wickedness in the heavenly places. Therefore take up the whole armor of God, that you may be able to withstand in the evil day, and having done all, to stand (Ephesians 6:10-13 NKJV).

The next five verses tell us about each piece of armor and its importance. When I get dressed every morning, I recite the armor of God. It's an easy and effective way for me to release my faith for God's protection on a daily basis. When I put on the helmet of salvation, I act as if I am putting on a helmet; then I put on the breastplate of righteousness, the belt of truth around my waist, my feet are shod with the preparation of the gospel of peace, and I pick up the shield of faith and the sword of the Spirit. Then I speak in tongues as verse 18 directs. Praying in the Spirit is the same as praying in tongues.

Stand therefore, having girded your waist with truth, having put on the breastplate of righteousness, and having shod your feet with the preparation of the gospel of peace; above all, taking the shield of faith with which you will be able to quench all the fiery darts of the wicked one. And take the helmet of salvation, and the sword of the Spirit, which is the word of God; praying always with all prayer and supplication in the Spirit, being watchful to this end with all perseverance and supplication for all the saints—and for me, that utterance may be given to me, that I may open my mouth boldly to make known the mystery of the gospel, for which I am an ambassador in chains; that

in it I may speak boldly, as I ought to speak
(Ephesians 6:14-20 NKJV).

I believe the pieces of the armor are equated to
an aspect of Jesus Christ. The helmet of salvation
is Jesus' death on the cross, which purchased salvation for all. The breastplate represents Christ's
righteousness that we receive as our own. Second
Corinthians 5:21 says that Jesus was made to be
sin for us so we could be righteousness of God in
Him. The belt of truth is found in John 14:6 where
Jesus tells us He is the way, the truth, and the
life. The shoes of peace represent the sharing of the
Gospel, the Good News of Jesus—He is the Prince
of Peace. The shield of faith is found in Hebrews
12:2: *"Looking unto Jesus the author and finisher of
our faith..."* The sword of the Spirit is the Word of
God, and Jesus is the Word come in the flesh (see
John 1:1). Then in Isaiah 58:8 it says that the glory
of the Lord will be your rear guard. Verse 11 says
that the Lord will guide you continually. This com-
pletes the armor of God.

The Lord's Prayer

The last weapon I want to mention here is the
Lord's Prayer. It's all inclusive of what you need,
and I often use it in warfare prayer: honoring the

Father God, for God's will to be done, forgiveness, financial provision, deliverance from evil. All of the basics of Christianity are covered.

Before I begin praying for specific needs, I often feel led to declare this prayer over my life, and in a group setting I have everyone pray the Lord's Prayer together. It confirms to those praying that they have spiritual authority in Christ and that the mighty power of God works through them. It's a great way to start a time of prayer.

> *After this manner therefore pray ye: Our Father which art in heaven, Hallowed be Thy name. Thy kingdom come, Thy will be done in earth, as it is in heaven. Give us this day our daily bread. And forgive us our debts, as we forgive our debtors. And lead us not into temptation, but deliver us from evil: For Thine is the kingdom, and the power, and the glory, for ever. Amen* (Matthew 6:9-13).

We Are in a Spiritual War

Whether believers realize it or not, we are all in a spiritual war and the enemy is the devil himself. God has given us the spiritual weapons we need to fight this enemy and we can win. He is the same devil Jesus defeated on Calvary. In the Old Testament when the children of Israel spoke of their enemies they had the promises of God to stand on. Today our enemies are in the demonic realm, but we can claim the same promises of victory for our battles. Galatians 3:29 gives us this promise: *"And if ye be Christ's, then are ye Abraham's seed, and heirs according to the promise."*

Remember this:

- God has given you many weapons to defeat the enemy and with the leading of the Holy Spirit you will know what to use in every situation.

- When you don't know what to do, pray in tongues and listen for the leading of God.

Chapter 9

Setting the Captives Free

I was a Spirit-filled pastor's wife and *captive* to a spirit of fear. I had no control over fear, and it was ruining my life. I had phobias about cancer, heights, water, and dying young—just to name a few. The enemy would use this against me in many ways. There were times I would feel as if a demonic force was going to push me down the steps and I would hold on as tight as I could to the railings. I recall on occasions being so afraid I could not open my mouth. Fear is torment: *"There is no fear in love; but perfect love casts out fear, because fear involves torment. But he who fears has not been made perfect in love"* (1 John 4:18 NKJV).

When I was first married, the enemy would harass me with fear about conversations I overhead as an eight-year-old child. My mother had died of complications from diabetes. I overheard the ladies of the church discuss why my mother died. They decided it was because my father was not saved and that my mother's death would drive him to the Lord. That's ridiculous, of course. Logically, it would be the opposite. He would need her to help him live the Christian life. But when I was older, the enemy brought this back up to me and told me I was the only other Christian in my family (at that time) and I would have to die for my father to be saved.

My husband was a great help to me at that time and told me Jesus died for my father and I didn't have to die for him. But that comfort would only last for a while and then the enemy would bring that fear on me again. I was even afraid to ride in the car with my father. I thought we would have a wreck and I would win him to the Lord with my dying breath. It sounds completely unreasonable now, but the enemy used that on me for a long time.

In our church we would pray at the altar after church on Sunday and Wednesday evenings. One night while I was praying at the altar, I wrestled with telling the Lord I would be willing to die for my father's salvation. It was so hard to pray that because I was just married and I wanted to have children. I finally did say I would be willing and I meant it. It freed me. The devil had nothing to harass me about any longer, at least on that point. The Lord sustained me through this torment of fear, but I knew I needed help. *"For God hath not given us the spirit of fear; but of power, and of love, and of a sound mind"* (2 Tim. 1:7).

Deliverance From Evil Spirits

At a pivotal point in my life, I was introduced to a lady who attended Bible school in New York and knew how to do deliverance. By the word *deliverance*, I mean she knew how to cast out evil spirits.

The Holy Spirit of God only comes into your life when He is invited, but evil spirits will come in uninvited when they see a crack in the door. One third of Jesus' ministry was casting out demons. Many Christians are afraid of this, but God has given us authority over demons and they must obey us in the name of Jesus. If there is an area of your life where you do not have control, it could be the work of a demon—anger, fear, worry, lust, anxiety, and others. God wants you to be free from these bondages, and as a Christian He wants you to know you have the authority to cast out demons.

A Christian cannot be possessed by demons, or wholly controlled by demons. But there can be certain areas where a demon can control a Christian. You could say they "oppress" Christians, but the terminology is not what is important. What's important is to be free. I was a Christian and a Spirit-filled one, but my life was controlled by a spirit of fear. The Lord sent someone into my life to help me and she did it by casting out a spirit of fear. My life changed immediately. I was free from many fears that had plagued me but not quite all of them.

Curiosity About Deliverance

The Lord gave me a great curiosity about deliverance after I met the lady from New York, and I began to do some research on my own. I read every book I could find on the subject. My pastor encouraged me, and Wilbur was interested as well. At that time, we had a tight group of Christians that would meet regularly for prayer. The Lord began to lead us by using the gift of discerning of spirits to cast out demons. When people would come to the group for prayer, God would show us if there was a demon involved. After some time, I realized our deliverance team could set me free from the fears that still bothered me. The team prayed over me and I stood on Second Timothy 1:7. I am free today! Jesus tells the disciples in Luke 10:17-19 they have power over satan:

*And the seventy returned again with joy,
saying, Lord, even the devils are subject unto
us through Thy name. And he said unto them,
I beheld Satan as lightning fall from heaven.
Behold, I give unto you power to tread on
serpents and scorpions, and over all the
power of the enemy: and nothing shall by any
means hurt you* (Luke 10:17-19).

Our First Experience

Before Wilbur and I started moving much in the
gifts of the Spirit, we had an experience where the
Lord used us in deliverance. Even though we were
not exactly sure what to do, the Lord led us with
the knowledge and understanding we had. We relied on the Word of knowledge and the Scriptures
we knew.

We were visiting some friends who lived in another state, and in the course of our conversation
we discovered their eight year old daughter would
not use her right arm. She said the devil told her
it belonged to him and she could not use it. We
ministered to her and made sure she had given her
heart to Jesus. Then we took authority over the enemy and commanded him to leave her alone. She
screamed so loud everyone in the house could hear

it, but she was set free that day. The enemy does not play fair and is so evil. He is a liar and the father of lies and often targets children. After we ministered to her, she could use her arm again. We led her in the Baptism of the Holy Spirit and she spoke with other tongues.

It's important when someone is delivered from an evil spirit that they fill the vacancy with the things of the Lord—prayer and reading God's Word. In Matthew 12 the Scriptures show us if the house (referring to a person) the demons were in is left empty, they will return and bring seven more demons with them. The state of the person would then be worse.

When the unclean spirit is gone out of a man, he walketh through dry places, seeking rest, and findeth none.

Then he saith, I will return into my house from whence I came out; and when he is come, he findeth it empty, swept, and garnished.

Then goeth he, and taketh with himself seven other spirits more wicked than himself, and they enter in and dwell there: and the last state of that man is worse than the first. Even so shall it be also unto this wicked generation (Matthew 12:43-45).

Growing in the Knowledge of God

We struggled in those early years without any mentor, but the Holy Spirit led us and each experience gave us confidence. As our understanding of our authority in Christ increased, we learned how to break the power of satan over people and situations much quicker. We all grew in the knowledge of God and in faith.

The discerning of spirits comes much easier now. In the years we have ministered this way, we have had all kinds of strange situations—people growled at us, tried to hit us, and answered back in tongues that were not of the Spirit of God. These attacks did not frighten us because we had learned we had authority in Christ. However, I think it would be very difficult if not impossible to do deliverance without having the baptism of the Holy Spirit with the evidence of speaking in tongues and the gifts of the Holy Spirit working in your life.

How to Begin

Before you begin to do deliverance, make sure everyone present asks the Lord to cleanse them with the blood of Jesus Christ and forgive them from any sins of word, thought, or deed. Be sure after the session to pray to cleanse your house inside and out, the air above and the earth beneath with the blood of Jesus Christ. When you cast out a demonic spirit, it will want to stay. Its desire is to find a person to live in or oppress. That is why it is so important to cleanse your house with the blood of Jesus.

Here's a sample of what I usually pray: "In the name of Jesus Christ, I command every evil spirit to leave my house. I plead the precious blood of Jesus over my house inside and outside, the air above and the earth beneath."

Read the Scriptures

I always start by reading the Scriptures in Mark 16. I read this passage out loud and I read Luke 10:18 and 19. Demons are legalistic and they must obey God's Word. I read the following Scriptures out loud for that very reason. Keep your Bible handy because you may need to refer to other Scriptures as the Lord leads you.

And He said unto them, Go ye into all the world, and preach the gospel to every creature.

He that believeth and is baptized shall be saved; but he that believeth not shall be damned.

And these signs shall follow them that believe; In My name shall they cast out devils; they shall speak with new tongues;

They shall take up serpents; and if they drink any deadly thing, it shall not hurt them; they shall lay hands on the sick, and they shall recover.

So then after the Lord had spoken unto them, He was received up into heaven, and sat on the right hand of God.

And they went forth, and preached every where, the Lord working with them, and confirming the word with signs following. Amen (Mark 16:15-20).

And He said to them, "I saw Satan fall like lightning from heaven. Behold, I give you the authority to trample on serpents and scorpions, and over all the power of the enemy, and nothing shall by any means hurt you" (Luke 10:18-19 NKJV).

In one account the man we were praying for said he had a problem with rage against his wife, even though she really didn't do anything to provoke it. The Lord reminded me of the Scripture in Proverbs 20:1 that says wine is a mocker and strong drink is raging. As soon as I read that verse, the man said, "Yes, the rage began when I started drinking!" Even though he was no longer drinking, the rage was still there. In this situation, I needed to refer to other Scriptures to pinpoint the problem. This is often the case.

Discerning of Spirits in Deliverance

The Lord tells me through discerning of spirits what demon is present. You can ask the Lord to reveal what demons are present. In some instances the person will already know and they will tell you. People usually know the areas they have problems in. They may not know the exact name of the demon, but the Lord will reveal it. If you still feel you do not know the name of the demon, you can just say what the demon does. You may say for instance, "Spirit that makes him angry". Always be listening to your spirit to what the Holy Spirit is saying, because there may be other demons present, not just one.

Remember you can test the Word that comes to you by asking that spirit to say Jesus came in the flesh according to First John 4:1-4. I wrote about this in detail in the chapter: Revelation Gifts, The Gift of Discerning of Spirits.

Renounce the Demons

The person who is receiving deliverance needs to renounce the demon. They must establish they do not want that demon any longer. In one instance we were praying with a girl who did not want to renounce the spirit of lust. We could not help her, because she was not in agreement. She allowed the demon to stay.

Bind the Strong Man

It is important to bind the strong man satan, first. Demons answer to satan so you bind him away first from the person receiving deliverance. Remember you cannot bind satan away from the whole world, just in the situation you are dealing with. I do it like this, "satan I bind you away from (person's name) in the name of Jesus Christ of Nazareth. Satan, you cancel every assignment against this person." The Scriptures for this are found in Luke 11:21-26 and Matthew 12:28-29.

When a strong man, fully armed, guards his own palace, his goods are in peace. But when a stronger than he comes upon him and overcomes him, he takes from him all his armor in which he trusted, and divides his spoils. He who is not with Me is against Me, and he who does not gather with Me scatters (Luke 11:21-23 NKJV).

But if I cast out demons by the Spirit of God, surely the kingdom of God has come upon you. Or how can one enter a strong man's house and plunder his goods, unless he first binds the strong man? And then he will spoil his house (Matthew 12:28-29).

In the Name of Jesus Christ of Nazareth

As mentioned in Chapter 6, when dealing with demons, always use the name of "Jesus Christ of Nazareth." We say "in the name of Jesus Christ of Nazareth" because that is how Peter and John spoke in Acts, chapter 3. This reference to Jesus' name differentiates Jesus our Lord from other people who are named "Jesus". Peter gives us an example of using Jesus' full name in the book of Acts: *"Then Peter said, 'Silver or gold I do not have, but what I have I give you. In the name of Jesus Christ of Nazareth, walk'"* (Acts 3:6 NIV).

Commanding Demons

The Bible tells us to lay hands on the sick, but when you cast out demons you speak to them or command them. You don't lay hands on the person. You command demons to come out just like Jesus did. You do not have to yell but you need to speak boldly with authority. An example can be found in Mark, chapter 9:

> *When Jesus saw that a crowd was running to the scene, He rebuked the evil spirit. "You deaf and mute spirit," He said, "I **command** you, come out of him and never enter him again"* (Mark 9:25 NIV).

And again He commands the evil spirits to come out in Luke, chapter 8.

> *For He had **commanded** the unclean spirit to come out of the man. For oftentimes it had caught him: and he was kept bound with chains and in fetters; and he brake the bands, and was driven of the devil into the wilderness* (Luke 8:29).

After you command the evil spirit to come out, then send them to the dry places where Jesus allows them to go and tell them not to come back. Then say, "The blood of Jesus Christ of Nazareth is against you."

We send evil spirits to dry places according to the Scriptures in Luke 11. Starting in verse 24, Jesus tells a story of an unclean spirit that went to the dry places seeking rest, but found none.

"When an unclean spirit goes out of a man, he goes through dry places, seeking rest; and finding none, he says, 'I will return to my house from which I came.' And when he comes, he finds it swept and put in order. Then he goes and takes with him seven other spirits more wicked than himself, and they enter and dwell there; and the last state of that man is worse than the first" (Luke 11:24-26 NKJV).

In this story, the last state of the man was worse because the man did not fill up with the Word of God and the demon came back with more demons. This is why you need to command them to go and not come back. You also need to counsel the person who has been set free to read the Word and pray on a regular basis.

Evil Manifestations

When a demon is cast out, they have to come out and they come out in various ways. It's important for you to know this so you are not surprised. Sometimes people cry or scream; sometimes they yawn; they may cough or blow them out. People who receive deliverance sometimes feel the demons come out of them, but that is not always the case. If a demon is hurting the person, you can command that demon to stop hurting them when they come out. When Jesus cast the demon out of the young boy in Luke, chapter 9, the demon threw the boy down and tore him, but Jesus rebuked the demon and the boy received deliverance: *"And as he was yet a coming, the devil threw him down, and tare him. And Jesus rebuked the unclean spirit, and healed the child, and delivered him again to his father"* (Luke 9:42).

Be Led by the Holy Spirit

These are the basics I have done and experienced in casting out demons, but you cannot put God in a formula. You need to always be attentive to the Holy Spirit and follow His leading. He may have you do something a little different than we have listed.

In some instances our team would praise the Lord and that would be the thing that drove the demons out. Sometimes the Lord would have us quote Scriptures. There were times when we just needed to command the demon to leave. It is so much fun to set the captive free! It is not scary at all. When people get set free, it is truly wonderful. We always celebrate and praise the Lord. Jesus truly sets us free: *"If the Son therefore shall make you free, ye shall be free indeed"* (John 8:36).

When you are working as a team, the Holy Spirit may anoint one to cast out the spirits and the others to pray. Then the Holy Spirit may change and the anointing will come on another member of the team. That gives the leader a rest and the others are able to participate in a greater way. Always follow the leading of the Holy Spirit.

Knowing Your Authority

Remember as a believer, you have authority over the devil. But don't attempt to do deliverance without someone to mentor you or to train you in this area unless the Lord leads you to do so. Make sure you choose a mentor who walks close to the Lord and knows the Scripture. If you don't know anyone like that, pray for God to send someone to you or ask God to teach you Himself. There are many books published specifically on this subject. Ask the Lord to lead you in which books to read.

In our early years many in our prayer team were attacked by the enemy in unusual ways. In some cases we were just blindsided. We did not understand all the precautions we needed to take in covering our families in the blood of Jesus and prayer. Always have someone to agree with you. You should not be doing it alone.

The Bible references the seven sons of Sceva (see Acts 19:14-17) who attempted to cast out demons, but the demons would not respect their authority. They did not know the Lord personally or understand the spiritual authority Jesus gave to those who received Him. They were beaten up by the demons:

> *Then certain of the vagabond Jews, exorcists, took upon them to call over them which had evil spirits the name of the LORD Jesus, saying, We adjure you by Jesus whom Paul preacheth.*

> *And there were seven sons of one Sceva, a Jew, and chief of the priests, which did so.*

*And the evil spirit answered and said, Jesus I
know, and Paul I know; but who are ye?*

*And the man in whom the evil spirit was
leaped on them, and overcame them, and
prevailed against them, so that they fled out
of that house naked and wounded.*

*And this was known to all the Jews and
Greeks also dwelling at Ephesus; and fear fell
on them all, and the name of the Lord Jesus
was magnified* (Acts 19:13-17).

Fasting and Deliverance

It's alright to fast before the time of deliverance,
but not right before or during deliverance. You really do need your strength. Be sure to eat something substantial before you cast out demons.

Deliverance and Sinners

It is useless to try to cast a demon out of a
sinner, unless that individual is going to receive
Jesus as his or her Lord and Savior. It would be
impossible for the sinner to stay free without the

Lord's help. You can, however, bind a demon so that it cannot influence that person for a short time. The person would not have to be saved or even know that you have bound the demon on his or her behalf. In that instance, the individual would experience what it is like to be free for a brief time. This could be the break needed to find lasting spiritual help.

There may be instances when the Lord impresses upon you that someone is being controlled by a demon and it is causing problems for you. It might be someone you know or someone you don't know who happens to be near you. You can bind that demon in Jesus' name to stop him from causing problems temporarily, but you cannot cast a demon out without that person's permission.

Knowing a Demonic Attack

I dropped in to visit Mary Ruth one day and when she opened the door she was moving very slowly. She had just come up steps from the basement and could hardly make it to the top. I asked her, "What is wrong with you?"

She said, "I feel like I'm dying!"

As Mary Ruth was talking she remembered she had prayed for someone's deliverance over the phone. She had forgotten to pray for protection through the blood of Jesus over her own house and life. We both recognized this was an open door for the enemy to come in. Those demons she had cast out came to her house. I commanded the spirit of death off of her in Jesus' name and we prayed over our families and our houses. After we prayed through, she was fine.

Jesus dealt with evil spirits in His ministry a great deal. There are nine examples of Jesus casting out demons in the Scriptures. He used His authority to cast out demons and He has given us that same authority. Be confident in who Christ has made you—an ambassador for Him and for the Kingdom of God. Acts 10:38 sums up the ministry of Jesus of whom we are an ambassador: *"How God anointed Jesus of Nazareth with the Holy Ghost and with power: who went about doing good, and healing all that were oppressed of the devil; for God was with Him."*

Jesus Encounters Demons

In three of the Gospels, the same instance of Jesus encountering a demon is listed: Matthew

8:28-34, Mark 5:1-20, and Luke 8:26-40. Matthew 8 says two are possessed with devils. Mark and Luke say one is possessed with devils. This is an excellent example of how Jesus responded to demons. Please take a moment to read the account from the Book of Luke.

And they arrived at the country of the Gadarenes, which is over against Galilee.

And when He went forth to land, there met Him out of the city a certain man, which had devils long time, and ware no clothes, neither abode in any house, but in the tombs.

When he saw Jesus, he cried out, and fell down before Him, and with a loud voice said, What have I to do with Thee, Jesus, Thou Son of God most high? I beseech Thee, torment me not.

(For He had commanded the unclean spirit to come out of the man. For oftentimes it had caught him: and he was kept bound with chains and in fetters; and he brake the bands, and was driven of the devil into the wilderness.)

And Jesus asked him, saying, What is thy name? And he said, Legion: because many devils were entered into him.

And they besought Him that He would not command them to go out into the deep.

And there was there an herd of many swine feeding on the mountain: and they besought Him that He would suffer them to enter into them. And He suffered them.

Then went the devils out of the man, and entered into the swine: and the herd ran violently down a steep place into the lake, and were choked.

When they that fed them saw what was done, they fled, and went and told it in the city and in the country.

Then they went out to see what was done; and came to Jesus, and found the man, out of whom the devils were departed, sitting at the feet of Jesus, clothed, and in his right mind: and they were afraid.

They also which saw it told them by what means he that was possessed of the devils was healed.

Then the whole multitude of the country of the Gadarenes round about besought Him to depart from them; for they were taken with great fear: and He went up into the ship, and returned back again.

Now the man out of whom the devils were departed besought Him that he might be with Him: but Jesus sent him away, saying,

Return to thine own house, and shew how great things God hath done unto thee. And he went his way, and published throughout the whole city how great things Jesus had done unto him.

And it came to pass, that, when Jesus was returned, the people gladly received Him: for they were all waiting for Him (Luke 8:26-40).

In all three accounts, the demons knew Jesus would cast them out, so they requested to be sent into the swine—2,000 of them. But the swine didn't want those demons either. They ran into the water and drowned. The financial loss from this incident made the villagers beg Jesus to leave. The reference of this story in Mark and Luke say the victim was crazy, unconquerable, naked, and lived in the cemetery. He cut himself with stones. He was in a terrible state! But even with all the demons—a legion which is 1,000—they could not keep the man from worshiping Jesus. After Jesus healed him, he asked Jesus if he could go with him, but Jesus said,

"Return to thine house, and shew how great things God hath done..." (Luke 8:39). The next verse stated that he returned home and published throughout the whole city the great things Jesus had done for him. When Jesus returned to that area, the people who had begged Jesus to leave were waiting for Him and gladly received Him.

What looked like a disaster to those people was in fact the key to the salvation of the city. For further Scripture references where Jesus cast out demons, please refer to the appendix in the back of the book.

Freedom Scriptures

The following Scriptures reveal how much God loves and cares for us. His desire is that we live in freedom, not under the oppression of the enemy. These Scriptures may be of use to you in spiritual warfare. Mark them in your Bible as well as the other Scriptures listed in this chapter and make a mental note of them to yourself.

Is not this the fast that I have chosen? to loose the bands of wickedness, to undo the heavy burdens, and to let the oppressed go free, and that ye break every yoke?

Is it not to deal thy bread to the hungry, and that thou bring the poor that are cast out to thy house? when thou seest the naked, that thou cover him; and that thou hide not thyself from thine own flesh?

Then shall thy light break forth as the morning, and thine health shall spring forth speedily: and thy righteousness shall go before thee; the glory of the Lord shall be thy reward.

Then shalt thou call, and the Lord shall answer; thou shalt cry, and He shall say, Here I am. If thou take away from the midst of thee the yoke, the putting forth of the finger, and speaking vanity;

And if thou draw out thy soul to the hungry, and satisfy the afflicted soul; then shall thy light rise in obscurity, and thy darkness be as the noon day:

And the LORD shall guide thee continually, and satisfy thy soul in drought, and make fat thy bones: and thou shalt be like a watered garden, and like a spring of water, whose waters fail not (Isaiah 58:6-11).

Happy is he that hath the God of Jacob for his help, whose hope is in the LORD his God:

Which made heaven, and earth, the sea, and all that therein is: which keepeth truth for ever:

Which executeth judgment for the oppressed: which giveth food to the hungry. The LORD looseth the prisoners:

The LORD openeth the eyes of the blind: the LORD raiseth them that are bowed down: the LORD loveth the righteous (Psalm 146:5-8).

Stand fast therefore in the liberty wherewith Christ hath made us free, and be not entangled again with the yoke of bondage (Galatians 5:1).

For the law of the Spirit of life in Christ Jesus hath made me free from the law of sin and death (Romans 8:2).

Remember This:

- Jesus gave you His authority over evil spirits. When you command them to leave, in the name of Jesus Christ of Nazareth, they must obey what you say.

- If you are new to dealing with evil spirits, pray with someone who has experience or in a group.

- Always plead or declare the blood of Jesus Christ over yourself, your family, and people who are present and their properties. It is very important to include everyone's property. The blood of Christ is powerful and faith in His blood protects you.

Chapter 10

Team Praying

Several years ago Wilbur and I were visiting friends on the east coast and during our visit Wilbur developed a pain in his side that would not go away. Wilbur has a very high pain tolerance and if he complains at all I know it is serious. We went to a local doctor and found out it was a kidney stone. It was quite large and the doctor said it was too big to pass. We wanted to get home to our doctor right away so Wilbur took pain pills until we could catch a flight home.

That Saturday night the prayer group was meeting at our house. Wilbur was still in pain and we determined to pray for him. One of our friends, Tim, felt that we all needed to pray in tongues and we did for quite awhile. Then he asked if anyone got a picture or a vision.

Two people said they saw a hammer. And I said, "Oh that is a Scripture: God's Word is like a hammer that breaks the rocks in pieces" (see Jer. 23:29).

Tim replied, "Go get a real hammer." We laid the hammer on Wilbur's back, gathered around him, and prayed. The pain left him immediately. He has not had a pain since. Several weeks after this incident, one of our friends from our prayer group, Sharon, bought a hammer and wrote Jeremiah 23:29 on it—the Scripture we stood on for Wilbur's healing. That hammer hangs on our living room wall today as a reminder of God's healing power. What a blessing we had those people of prayer around us when we needed them. Ecclesiastes chapter 4 tells us how important it is to have people stand with us in battle: *"And if one prevail against him, two shall withstand him; and a threefold cord is not quickly broken"* (Eccles. 4:12).

The Body of Christ

There is great value in having a team of people praying together. We are the Body of Christ and the Body has many members, each with different gifts. First Corinthians chapter 12 shows just how important each part of the Body of Christ is and how important it is for us to work together. Verse 27 in the New International Version sums it up by saying, *"Now you are the body of Christ, and each one of you is a part of it."*

The Holy Spirit gives various gifts as He wills and they are used differently with different people. In our prayer group Becky receives visions, Mary Ruth and I interpret them, all of us agree in prayer, and pray until the burden lifts. Ester reads the Scriptures needed and Wilbur ministers as he's led by the Spirit. You can see how much we can accomplish when we pray together. Praying through together is so rewarding. The Holy Spirit leads us in an adventure as we discover the answers. It is fun and we often laugh as the revelations come.

Praying Together Is Powerful

We have discussed the prayer of agreement in an earlier chapter but I want to reiterate that it is so powerful. When you pray with other believers your confidence in prayer grows strong and it gives you an opportunity to move in the gifts of the Spirit. You can accomplish so much more in your prayer time when you come together with other believers. Matthew 18:19 tells us if we agree about anything, it will be done: *"Again, I tell you that if two of you on earth agree about anything you ask for, it will be done for you by My Father in heaven"* (Matt. 18:19 NIV).

Please note the Scripture says "anything," not "anyone." God has given people a free will and God will not violate their will. You can pray about people and take authority over the evil spirits that may be influencing them, but you cannot make decisions for them. Their decisions are subject to their own will. However, you can pray and agree about "things" or circumstances and stand on this verse.

Visions From God

Often the Holy Spirit leads me to have everyone in the prayer group ask the Lord for a vision. I call them darkly pictures after the Scripture First Corinthians 13:12, *"For now we see through a glass, darkly; but then face to face: now I know in part; but then shall I know even as also I am known."*

The Lord gives me the interpretation of each of the visions together. They would seem to be unrelated in our natural thinking, but the Holy Spirit brings them all together as a Word of encouragement to the group. No human could do that, only the Holy Spirit. On one occasion in prayer, the Lord gave me a color for each of our children and an interpretation of that color. Each one fit that child to the tee. The Lord often used pictures in the Scriptures to illustrate principles. Pictures are so much easier to remember than words.

The Fragrance of the Lord

Several times in group praying we have smelled the fragrance of Jesus. It is wonderful—very delicate and non-offensive. The first time this happened, six of us were returning home from an Aglow conference in Rapid City. A fragrance like that of roses filled the car. We had been praying and singing praise songs for about five hours as we drove. In another incident four ladies were praying with me in my kitchen. We had prayed for some time that day. A beautiful fragrance came into the room on a soft breeze. In another experience after a great time of prayer, my friend Becky had prayed for Mary Ruth and myself what she calls a "soaking prayer." She prays for about 10 or 15 minutes over one person until she feels a release—she has prayed through. We all felt a breeze come into the room after that and then a wonderful fragrance of vanilla followed. It was very strong and stayed quite awhile.

Singing the Scriptures

When we are meeting together for prayer and sharing, often a thought from one of the group will remind me of a song or a chorus. The Holy Spirit leads me this way, and when I have this prompting, we sing that song.

During the revival or charismatic renewal in the 1970s, Christians were singing the Scriptures, many times out of the Psalms. We often do that in our prayer groups even today. Singing the Scriptures is a beautiful way to welcome in the presence of the Holy Spirit. You know you are singing things that please Him when you sing the Scriptures. Some of the Scriptures we often sing are Psalm 19:7-10, 14; Psalm 34:1-4; Psalm 37:23-24; Psalm 91:1-2; Psalm 100; Acts 3:3-8; Isaiah 51:11; Isaiah 61:3; and Revelation 4:11.

Prayer and Share Groups

In our prayer groups people share and we have prayer about the needs in the group. We call our method, "prayer and share groups." We are always sure we have Scriptures and prayer. We pray with people for their needs and often the Lord gives individuals a specific Word. It is so encouraging to fellowship around the Lord. It builds all of us up and helps us to live in victory even on the days when we don't meet.

Sometimes in our prayer group we take communion. My husband has the Scriptures about communion memorized (see 1 Corinthians 11:23-29). We believe for physical healing when we take the bread representing Jesus' body and we remember how Jesus died for our sins and cleansed us so we can be free.

Wilbur and I are also involved in our local church. As we surround ourselves with believers, we become strong and bold for the Lord. We bear one another's burdens (see Gal. 6:2), rejoice together in answered prayer, and love one another in Christ. The Word admonishes us to get together often and encourage one another. This is so important in your Christian walk. If you do not have a group of Christians to fellowship with, ask the Lord to give you some Christian friends and prayer partners. The apostle Paul admonishes us to meet together in Hebrews 10:25: *"Let us not give up meeting together, as some are in the habit of doing, but let us encourage one another—and all the more as you see the Day approaching"* (NIV).

Remember This:

- Praying in a group is powerful according to Matthew 18:19; where two or three agree on anything in the name of Jesus, it will be done by the Father in Heaven.

- The Body of Christ has many members and all are important. As you pray together, God is able to use the gifts He has given each one to help the others. It's an exciting adventure to be able to use your gifts for God's glory.

Chapter 11

Healing Prayer

During one summer Wilbur was tearing down an old building to clear some land when an old nail hit him directly in his eye. He came home immediately and asked me to call the doctor. He could only see light and dark out of that eye. On the way to the doctor Wilbur remembered one of the churches in town was having special meetings with an evangelist. We took a detour from the doctor and stopped at church for prayer. The evangelist took one look and said that he had just prayed for a man in Seattle with the very same type of injury—a shattered lens. The man was healed! The evangelist prayed for Wilbur and Wilbur could see instantly. We cancelled the doctor's appointment. Wilbur could read the road signs on the way home and after two weeks of an inflamed eye, he had no permanent damage. Praise God for His healing power and provision.

During Jesus' earthly ministry, the Bible records numerous healings and in fact in every incident but one, Jesus heals them all! The only time He does a "few miracles" is in His hometown, because of their unbelief. This same Jesus is alive today and sitting at the right hand of the Father God. He is still our Healer. The book of Matthew records His amazing power: *"But when Jesus knew it, He withdrew Himself from thence: and great multitudes followed Him, and He healed them all"* (Matt. 12:15).

Jesus bought and paid for our physical healing by the 39 stripes He received from the whipping before he was crucified. Isaiah 53 prophesies of this event and tells of Jesus' healing power:

> *Surely He hath borne our griefs, and carried our sorrows: yet we did esteem Him stricken, smitten of God, and afflicted. But He was wounded for our transgressions, He was bruised for our iniquities: the chastisement of our peace was upon Him; and with His stripes we are healed* (Isaiah 53:4-5).

Healing for Conception

My mother was told she could not have children. When she began to gain weight in her womb from the baby, she would miscarry. At that time she was a part of a ladies' prayer group. One of the ladies went out of town and received the baptism of the Holy Spirit and of course they all wanted it then. The church they attended had an intern pastor who said part of the Bible was true and part of it was not true. My Aunt Sadie stood up, held her Bible up and said, "I'll have you know that every Word in this book is true." In two weeks all the Spirit-filled believers were asked to leave that church. Most of the leadership left as well.

God turned it for good however, because they started the first Pentecostal church in South Dakota. The pastor of the new church anointed my mother with oil and prayed for her healing. I was born within a year and then my sister was born three years later. James 5:14 instructs us to anoint with oil: *"Is any one of you sick? He should call the elders of the church to pray over him and anoint him with oil in the name of the Lord"* (James 5:14 NIV).

Healing and Doctors

There were times when Wilbur and I were healed just through prayer, but there have also been times when we received healing by going to the doctor. In each case we had to listen to the Spirit of God and follow after the peace in our hearts. In all of these instances, we have relied on the power of prayer to see us through. Several years ago Wilbur had heart surgery. I called all of our prayer partners to agree with us and we could feel the prayers surrounding us. It was a complicated surgery but Wilbur came through and has had no further trouble.

Many years ago, I tested positive for cancer. I needed surgery and Wilbur and I felt that we should proceed that way. When I was in the operating room, I prayed and the Lord gave me a vision of a train going over a precipice. Then He said, "When you need Me, I will be there like the bridge was over the precipice for the train." I recovered completely. The book of Isaiah gives us this promise:

When you pass through the waters, I will be with you; and through the rivers, they shall not overflow you. When you walk through the fire, you shall not be burned, nor shall the flame scorch you (Isaiah 43:2 NKJV).

We have had many more instances of healing of which I could probably fill another book, but what is important is that you understand the power of prayer in regards to healing. Let God lead you instead of relying on your own wisdom. Trust in Him as Proverbs 3:5-8 tells us:

Trust in the LORD with all your heart, and lean not on your own understanding; In all your ways acknowledge Him, and He shall direct your paths. Do not be wise in your own eyes; fear the LORD and depart from evil. It will be health to your flesh, and strength to your bones (NKJV).

The Wrong Way to Pray

I had trouble getting pregnant just like my mother. At first I prayed, "Don't let me have a baby if it will grow up and not be saved and go to hell." I told my mother-in-law how I prayed and she said, "Do not pray that way! Instead pray: Lord, give me a baby and help me to raise them for you." I changed my prayer and shortly after that I became pregnant and we had a son! But my son was followed by two miscarriages. The doctor told me that I would never have any more children. But God had another idea.

Believe When You Pray

I read a book in my early years that significantly changed the way I thought about healing. It taught on Mark 11:24 emphasizing the phrase, *"when you pray."* Jesus taught the disciples to believe when they prayed, not when they saw it happen. In the chapter Jesus was hungry and found a fig tree, but there were no figs on it. He cursed the fig tree, but nothing immediately happened. However, the next day when the disciples passed the tree again, it had died. Jesus used this instance to teach them how to believe in what they say regardless of what they see at the time.

In the same respect as a believer praying for healing, we are to believe we receive healing when we pray, not some time in the future. This passage is found in Mark 11:24: *"Therefore I say unto you, What things soever ye desire, when ye pray, believe that ye receive them, and ye shall have them"* (Mark 11:24).

I also made a "Hannah promise" when I asked the Lord for a child. In First Samuel, chapter 1, a story is recorded of a woman named Hannah. Hannah could not have any children and her husband's other wife would continually throw this up in her face. Hannah cried out to God for a son and told Him that she would give the son to the Lord if she could have one. Shortly after she made that promise she became pregnant and had a son named Samuel. She kept her promise sending her son to be trained under the priest Eli. She had several more children after Samuel was born. This kind of promise is often referred to as a "Hannah promise".

I did have a child after I made that promise, but I was very young at the time and I would not recommend making a "vow" like that today because that type of prayer is under the Old Testament. God worked with me where I was—I had faith to believe. Today, however, we have a better covenant under the blood of Jesus Christ. I recommend standing on Mark 11:24.

A Day of Rest

When I became pregnant with our second son, the Lord guided me through the advice of others that I needed to rest. Part of my healing I believe, came through letting my body rest. Wilbur and I had been working seven days a week for eight years not realizing everyone needs a day of rest. One doctor thought I miscarried because of overwork, and Wilbur was so stressed that he had broken out in a rash.

I was so hopeless about having more children that I began making plans to go back to college and become a school teacher, but the Lord had a better way. One of the Ten Commandments is to remember the Sabbath day to keep it holy. God made us to have a day of rest.

God's Promise of Conception

My second pregnancy was difficult, but we had gone back to my home church and my pastors prayed for me. I experienced many small healings while I was pregnant. Exodus 23 gives us an important promise regarding children. If you or someone you know had has trouble conceiving, this is a powerful verse to stand on:

> *And ye shall serve the LORD your God, and He shall bless thy bread, and thy water; and I will take sickness away from the midst of thee. There shall nothing cast their young, nor be barren, in thy land: the number of thy days I will fulfill* (Exodus 23:25-26).

After our son was born, I asked the Lord for a daughter. She was born two years later. Then I thought she needed a sister and I planned to get serious and pray for that, but before I asked my youngest daughter was on the way!

Levels of Prayer

Matthew 7:7-8 describes the levels of prayer ranging from easy to difficult to answer. The

Scripture says you must ask, seek, and knock. Sometimes you just have to ask, other times it may take some seeking God for the answer, and sometimes you may need to knock on the door before it is opened:

> *Ask, and it shall be given you; seek, and ye shall find; knock, and it shall be opened unto you:*

> *For every one that asketh receiveth; and he that seeketh findeth; and to him that knocketh it shall be opened* (Matthew 7:7-8).

For instance, a more difficult prayer may be when you are praying specifically for a person's salvation. That person's free will is involved and they must choose Christ. Your prayers may be ongoing for them.

In Luke 18 Jesus tells the disciples a parable to show them they must pray and not give up. A widow persisted with a judge until she received her request. On the other hand, there is also the Scripture in Isaiah 6:24 which says God will answer before you ask. In my experience, I have had to pray all these ways to receive answers. You must pray how you feel led in each situation because every one of them is different and you don't know all of the underlying circumstances. You must trust God. James 5:16 shows us that our answer will come: *"The earnest (heartfelt, continued) prayer of a righteous man makes tremendous power available [dynamic in its working]"* (James 5:16 AMP).

Long Life

Wilbur and I had been pastors in town for several years, but we lived and farmed with my father to supplement our income. We helped the church get its own building. The church had grown, and the building was finally paid off. My father was getting older and Wilbur felt that it was time for the church to have a full-time pastor who could live in town. Wilbur said to me, "There are a lot of others who can preach, but we are the only ones who can help your father."

I had felt the call of the Lord on my life so I did not know what to do about leaving the ministry. We had experienced persecution by our peers and were treated as if we had backslidden because we were no longer pastors. However, we won more souls to the Lord, out of the ministry, just being ordinary Christians. We joined the Gideons, Full Gospel Businessmen's Fellowship, and Aglow—plus we were involved in our local church. God's real plan for us was much better than what I thought was His plan for us. I was involved with a ladies interfaith coffee for many years and also had a women's prayer and share group in my home. We had the privilege and joy of living with my father and still did valuable work for the Lord. The Bible tells us to honor your father and mother and you will live long in the land. It's one of the Ten Commandments and the first commandment God gave us with a promise: *"Honor your father and your mother, that your days may be long upon the land which the LORD your God is giving you"* (Exod. 20:12 NKJV).

Remember this:

- Jesus Christ paid the price for the healing of our bodies when he suffered and died on the cross.

- In Mark 11:24-25 Jesus taught us to believe we receive when we pray, not sometime in the future. Even if you don't see circumstances change, you stay in faith that you received your healing.

- God has given us the promise of conception and you can believe Him for children.

- God sometimes works through doctors, medicine, and surgery to bring healing. Always seek His guidance and listen for his direction inside.

Chapter 12

Humble Yourself

In the early '90s, I was appointed as the state prayer chairman of Women's Aglow. This was a new position created as a result of a deliberate prayer thrust for the Aglow organization. Because I loved Aglow and I loved to pray, I was thrilled to accept.

One of my responsibilities was to attend the National Aglow Conference and that year I went to the conference held in Washington, D.C. Wilbur said I must go and it took several financial miracles for me to attend.

As a prayer chairman I was given a copy of the book, *Taking Our Cities for God* by John Dawson.[1] I was remarkably impressed by the author's account of taking 200 YWAM (Youth With A Mission) volunteers to Cordoba, Argentina, South America. It was a proud and beautiful city with people who put much importance on position, appearance, and possessions. The street meetings and evangelistic outreaches were met with cold indifference by the citizens of Cordoba.

John Dawson called for a day of fasting and prayer. As they prayed in groups of about 20, the Lord simultaneously revealed to several groups the ruling principality or spirit over the city was the spirit of pride. The Lord also revealed a strategy for pulling down the stronghold over the city—to show the humility of Christ through personal humility.

The group went down to a popular shopping mall, kneeled down on the cobblestones with their foreheads on the street, and prayed for the city. When John Dawson arose to his feet, his intimidation was gone. He explained to the crowd that had gathered why Youth with a Mission had come to Cordoba. Many people responded to the message and received the literature and even stood patiently in line to have the tracts autographed![2]

Personal Humility

This amazing incident caused me to consider a personal situation in my own life. Wilbur and I had reached a stalemate in the negotiations to lease our farmland. I discussed this with my youngest son and he responded, "Well, I can humble myself."

I replied, "Well, I can humble myself, too." Together we laid facedown on the floor and prayed. Our position was symbolic of the humility in our hearts. True humility comes from yielding our wills in total submission and obedience to God. Within two weeks the contract was signed to the satisfaction of all.

My sister Mary Ruth and her husband were negotiating a lease for their property as well. Two months passed and they were still not able to come to terms. Mary Ruth and I humbled ourselves before the Lord and prayed for a resolution. In two weeks, the contract was signed. Why did we wait so long?

Not long after these incidents, my youngest son and his wife were preparing to graduate from our local university. My son did not have a job yet and his wife would soon deliver their third child. I suggested we humble ourselves before the Lord and ask for a job for my son in a prosperous city where they wanted to move. We all got down on the floor and prayed. Within three days he was offered a great position in that city. First Peter 5 illustrates this principle for us:

Likewise ye younger submit yourselves to the elder. Yea, all of you be subject one to another and be clothed with humility: for God resisteth the proud, and giveth grace to the humble. Humble yourselves therefore under the mighty hand of God, that He may exalt you in due time (1 Peter 5:5-6).

How many times do we struggle with situations in our life and not even stop to pray and ask God to help? And when we do pray—are we praying with humility? God honors a sincere heart and a prayer spoken in faith in order that He can intervene in our affairs and make all the difference. Again the Scriptures tell us: *"Humble yourselves in the sight of the Lord, and He shall lift you up"* (James 4:10).

Did you notice that the Bible says to humble *yourself*? You do not need to pray for the Lord to humble you. You do it yourself. You make a decision of your free will to humble yourself and God honors that.

Breakthroughs in Prayer

A week after my son received the job offer, my friend Karen stopped in for prayer at my sister's house. Her son, Quentin, was in a similar situation of needing a job. I told her about my son's answer to prayer and all of us humbled ourselves before the Lord and prayed. We laid flat on our faces on the floor as an act of humility. When we got up, my sister prophesied where Quentin's job would be. In three days Quentin had a job in that very city and his fiancée also found one nearby.

I could go on to tell you many other incidents of answered prayers when we humbled ourselves before the Lord—financial miracles, employment opportunities, salvation of loved ones, and more. Every opportunity I have, I tell this story and people get down on the floor with me in humility and pray. I am so thankful for John Dawson's book and for those who donated the book to the Aglow prayer chairmen. The ripple effects have happened everywhere I tell these amazing stories of the good things God has done for us. It's like the small lunch from the little boy that, when placed in the hands of Jesus, fed the multitude. What we have may not seem like enough, but then Jesus blesses it, and it becomes more than adequate.

Humility in the Bible

There are many accounts in the Bible that show us the power of humility. Elijah put his head between his knees when he prayed for rain on Mt. Carmel (see 1 Kings 18:42). Jesus humbled Himself in the Garden of Gethsemane to yield to the will of His Father (see Matthew 26:39). The whole trial and scourging and Crucifixion shows how Jesus allowed Himself to be humbled in front of many people (see Matthew 26-27). The nobleman humbled himself to ask Jesus to heal his son in Matthew 8:5-13. Zacchaeus was a rich tax collector who humbled himself and climbed a tree in order to see Jesus (see Luke 19:2-10). And there are many other incidents in the Old and New Testaments. What a powerful concept this is and important for us to remember in prayer.

Remember this:

- The Scriptures tell us God resists the proud but gives grace to the humble (see 1 Peter 5:5-6). Always put yourself in a place of humility when coming to the Lord.

- Sometimes an act can be a powerful way to express your humility—bowing down or even laying flat on the floor.

- The Lord does not humble you; you must humble yourself as an act of your will (see James 4:10).

Endnotes

1. John Dawson, *Taking Our Cities for God* (Lake Mary, FL: Creation House, 2001).

2. Ibid.

Chapter 13

Protection

When our son was in high school, he was driving—enough said. For all those parents whose kids are beginning to drive, I can say that the power of God's protection is a wonderful thing to rely on. On one particular day my son had just left for school when I heard the train whistle. The train ran about a mile from our house and the train crossing only had a sign—no flashing lights or security bar. As soon as I heard that train whistle I had a burden to pray for him. I pled the blood of Jesus Christ right then and prayed through until the burden lifted. When he got home that day, I asked him about it. He was driving a noisy pickup with the radio on. He looked up just in time and slammed on the brakes. The train roared by right in front of him.

Protection from God is a wonderful promise, and we need it in the world we live in. I make it a habit to plead the blood of Jesus Christ over myself, my family, and our home every day. I also pray that the Lord will order my steps according to His Word: *"The steps of a good man are ordered by the LORD: and He delighteth in his way"* (Ps. 37:23).

I also put on the armor of God according to Ephesians 6:10-18 and pray in the Spirit. I have a place in my day to release my faith for God's protection and my confidence is secure. I've given the Lord permission to order my day and everything goes better when I do that.

Protection From Storms

When my two middle children were in grade school, I took them and two other children from the church to a weeklong youth camp in Iowa. While I was cleaning the house before my cousin was to visit, a burden hit me about the weather over the camp. I could not pray through so I called my pastor's wife to pray too.

In our part of the country, a tornado always moves from the southwest and goes to the northeast. A tornado was heading straight for the kid's campground that day and the staff had everyone in the most sturdy building there. They were all praying and we were praying and praying in the Spirit.

All of a sudden, the tornado turned and went another direction, sparing the camp and leaving them with just heavy rains. The promises of God for protection have been given to us, but we must release our faith in them. And to do that, we need to know those Scriptures: *"The righteous cry out, and the LORD hears, and delivers them out of all their troubles"* (Ps. 34:17 NKJV).

Provision for Protection

Our family traveled to Portland every year to visit Wilbur's relatives. One year before we left on the trip, Mary Ruth had a burden for us. As we traveled into Oregon on those steep and winding roads, I also had a burden to pray. I prayed and prayed but the burden remained. One of our nephews was with us on that trip and he became sick from the car motion. We stopped to give him some relief. When we started again, the transmission had gone out of our car! Since we were heading downhill at that point, we were able to coast to a garage.

The mechanics told us the car had to stay above 30 mph or we would be stuck. We were so close to Portland at that point we decided to take the car all the way in. I ran to the grocery store to get picnic type food because we could not stop. We ate in the car on the way. The mechanics gave us a push to get us started and by taking back roads we were able to arrive at our destination. Wilbur and his brother put a new transmission in the car while we were there so we could get home safely. The Lord's provision was there for our protection. God's promise to us is in Philippians 4:19: *"But my God shall supply all your need according to His riches in glory by Christ Jesus."*

Protection With Grace and Mercy

Our son and Mary Ruth's son were about ten years old and decided to climb the silo and walk around the top. The silo was 40 feet tall and the bricks were only 6 inches thick! They decided part of the way around to sit down and scoot on the way back to the ladder. Those kids did many dangerous things I did not know about until they were grown. Praise God for His grace and mercy over our children. Those prayers may not seem like they are doing anything at the time, but you may find after many years they made a valuable difference. Psalm 32:10 tells us of God's great mercy: *"Many sorrows shall be to the wicked: but he that trusteth in the LORD, mercy shall compass him about"* (Ps. 32:10).

My friend Beverly owns a farm in Tennessee. Her daughter and a friend were riding horses one afternoon when they both got extremely thirsty. They decided to turn back and go to the house to get a drink. Before they got inside the house, they heard a very loud, terrifying sound. They looked up and saw a tornado coming right at them. They ran into the house and got in the bathroom. The tornado took out all the barns on the farm. The house lost its roof and all the windows were blown out, but those girls were safe. Beverly believes it was the Lord who gave them the incredible thirst that day and it was God that saved their lives.

Protection of the Lord comes in many ways. It's important to keep in fellowship with Him so you hear His voice clearly on the inside. He can help you in ways you have not even dreamed. Isaiah 55 tells us that the Lord's thoughts are higher than our thoughts; we need to listen:

For My thoughts are not your thoughts, neither are your ways My ways, saith the LORD. For as the heavens are higher than the earth, so are My ways higher than your ways, and My thoughts than your thoughts (Isaiah 55:8-9).

Remember this:

- God promises His children protection. When you sincerely plead or declare the blood of Jesus over yourself, your family, your home and property, you actively release your faith for God's protection.

- Always be aware of the leading of the Holy Spirit. Often a knowing in your spirit is God letting you know to change your situation.

Chapter 14

Hearing God's Voice

When I was a little girl, I was looking out the north window of my Aunt Sadie's living room. The Holy Spirit spoke inside my spirit. Even though I did not know Him very well at that time, He told me I would go to Bible college for three years and then get married. I didn't even realize then it was God's voice. Later after I graduated from high school my pastor, Bernard Ridings, asked me if I would like to go to Bible school. I had not even thought about going to Bible school, but as soon as he said it, I knew I should go because the Lord had told me years before. I said, "Yes!" First Corinthians 2:9-10 shows us God wants us to know the good things He has for us:

> But as it is written, Eye hath not seen, nor ear heard, neither have entered into the heart of man, the things which God hath prepared for them that love Him. But God hath revealed them unto us by His Spirit: for the Spirit

searcheth all things, yea, the deep things of
God (1 Corinthians 2:9-10).

Pastor Ridings spoke to me in July of that year and at that time many men had just come back from World War II making enrollment higher. I didn't even know how to apply for college, but my pastor helped me with all the details. He got me into school even though there was no room in the dormitory. My mother died when I was eight years old, but the Lord sent others to help me. The Lord was always gently pushing me toward my destiny.

Obedience Brings Provision

Pastor Ridings asked his mother-in-law if she would let me stay with her until the dormitory had an opening. His mother-in-law was Mrs. Sarah Crouch, mother of the Paul Crouch, who went on to establish the Trinity Broadcasting Network. Paul was in grade school at the time and was a thoughtful and gracious person, even as a boy. He always made sure I had enough to eat. Mrs. Crouch sewed my uniforms and was such a blessing to me. Mrs. Crouch, Paul, and his sister Ruth spent a winter with Pastor Ridings and his wife Naomi in my hometown and so I was familiar with their family. Naomi was the oldest daughter in the family and Ruth the youngest daughter. Ruth has always been a dear friend and stood up in my wedding. The Lord provided this divine connection in my life for provision when I needed it. Proverbs 14:26 declares this promise: *"In the fear of the LORD is strong confidence: and His children shall have a place of refuge."*

If the Lord had not told me in my childhood days I would go to Bible school, I would not have known. My father objected to my going so far away when we had a university within a few miles, but eventually my father agreed to let me go and paid for everything I needed, including the bus ride. Central Bible Institute is where I met my wonderful husband, Wilbur. The Holy Spirit had led Wilbur there by just "a knowing" he needed to come. He could have farmed in his home state of Idaho, but after being in the Air Force for four years and away from church, he felt he needed to catch up on his spiritual life. We have enjoyed the relationships we made during those college years all of our lives. When God is directing your life, His provision is there for you. Philippians 4:19 in the New Living Translation promises God will take care of us: *"And this same God who takes care of me will supply all your needs from His glorious riches, which have been given to us in Christ Jesus."*

I want you to keep in mind here that my mother-in-law knew how to pray through and had prayed for her family all those years. My mother, even though she died prematurely, was also a godly woman and spent much time at the altar. I believe those prayers laid the foundation for my life. Never underestimate the power of prayer.

You Can Hear From God

Hearing God's voice yourself is important for every believer. God wants us to know Him. As you read God's Word, His character is revealed to you. You can "hear" Him through His Word. Then when He speaks to you in your spirit about more specific things, you recognize His voice. Jesus gives an analogy to the disciples in John 10:2-5 that promises us we can know the voice of God:

> But he that entereth in by the door is the shepherd of the sheep. To him the porter openeth; and the sheep hear his voice: and he calleth his own sheep by name, and leadeth them out. And when he putteth forth his own sheep, he goeth before them, and the sheep follow him: for they know his voice. And a stranger will they not follow, but will

*flee from him: for they know not the voice of
strangers* (John 10:2-5).

In this parable, Jesus is the door to the
sheepfold and the sheep go in to the Father God
through Jesus. The sheep recognize the Father's
voice. When you accepted Jesus as your Lord,
He became the mediator between you and the
Father God. Because of Jesus, you can converse
with the Father freely. God wants to fellowship
with you. As much as you will allow Him, He will
be involved in your life. By staying in the Word
of God and by keeping constant communication
open with God every day, you begin to recognize
when the Lord is speaking to you, when the enemy is speaking to you, and when it is just your
own will.

Isaiah 58:11 declares the Lord will guide you
continually. Psalm 32:8 says He will instruct you
and guide you with his eye. Isaiah 30:20-21 says
you will hear with your ear a word behind you saying go neither to the right nor to the left and Psalm
37:23-24 says the steps of good men are ordered
by the Lord. All of these verses would benefit you
greatly—mark them in your Bible and memorize
them. Then when you need to make a decision, recite those Scriptures and release your faith that
you *can* hear God's voice.

God's Wisdom Comes With Peace

On one occasion Wilbur and I were considering borrowing money for our farm from a recommended source. The Lord spoke to me unexpectedly one day when I was just waking up that we should not make an alliance with that source. It was a warning so we did not pursue that course. It was not an audible voice, but it was clear to me in my spirit. Wilbur was in agreement with me and we chose another route. James 3:17 shows us that God's wisdom is peaceful and gentle:

> But the wisdom that is from above is first pure, then peaceable, gentle, and easy to be intreated, full of mercy and good fruits, without partiality, and without hypocrisy.

God is never harsh with us. When He gives us a warning, it still comes with peace.

The Inner Witness

Hearing God's voice could be a knowing or strong impression or it could come like a Word of knowledge with specific instructions. Jesus is the Prince of Peace and He left His peace with us to lead us according to John 14:25-27:

All this I have spoken while still with you. But the Counselor, the Holy Spirit, whom the Father will send in My name, will teach you all things and will remind you of everything I have said to you. Peace I leave with you; My peace I give you. I do not give to you as the world gives. Do not let your hearts be troubled and do not be afraid (John 14:25-27 NIV).

Jesus also sent the Holy Spirit to help us. He leads us by an inner witness, because He is in us: *"And let the peace of God rule in your hearts, to which also you were called in one body; and be thankful"* (Col. 3:15 NKJV).

An Audible Voice

Hearing God's voice could be audible, but He usually chooses to lead us by peace in our hearts. The peace of God cannot be imitated by the devil, but signs and circumstances may be. Even if you do hear an audible voice, always check it in your spirit. I know one friend who heard her name called out loud. She was young and had not heard about the Lord. She looked for a church after that and has always lived for the Lord. I know another woman who was called into the ministry with an audible voice, but in both cases, the audible voice was confirmed by peace in their hearts.

An Open and Shut Door

If you are still confused about which direction to go, you can pray for guidance by an open and shut door found in Revelation 3:8: *"I know your works. See, I have set before you an open door, and no one can shut it; for you have a little strength, have kept My word, and not denied My name"* (NKJV).

After seeking after God's peace, I will let the Lord know I am going to pursue a course of action. I ask Him to shut the door on that opportunity if I am not to pursue it. As I begin to move forward in that course of action, I pay close attention to the peace of God in my spirit (see Col. 3:15). If I begin to have an uneasiness in my spirit, then I stop and go back to the Lord in prayer.

Three Lights

Before I could hear God's voice, I used this as a rule of thumb, and I often tell young people about this for decision making. There are three pilot lights on the Columbia River. If they all line up in a row, the channel is safe from sand bars and the boats can proceed.

In prayer I think of that example as this: the first light is if the Lord approves of your decision. For instance, you would know it is not God's will for you to apply for a job in a liquor store. It would not be good for the Kingdom of God so the answer would be "no." The second light is if the circumstances work out. I want to say here, however, you should be in prayer about the circumstances because the enemy can come in and cause problems. The third light is inner peace. Satan cannot imitate the peace of God.

When all three of these areas line up, you can feel assured you are moving in the direction God has for you. If you get a red light, then stop and go back to the Lord in prayer. God sometimes answers differently than we would like. There is a saying that the Lord never takes anything away from you but that He gives you something more and better back. I have found that always to be true in my own life.

Walk Close to the Lord

It is important to walk close to the Lord and keep your life clean from sin to hear Him effectively. King David wrote in Psalm 66:18: *"If I regard iniquity in my heart, the Lord will not hear me*" (Ps. 66:18).Solomon wrote in Proverbs 28:13: "*He that covereth his sins shall not prosper; but whoso confesseth and forsaketh them shall have mercy.*" The prophet Isaiah wrote in Isaiah 59:2: "*Your inquities have separated between you and your God, and your sins have hid His face from you, that He will not hear.*" Verse 12 says: "*For our transgressions are multiplies before Thee, and our sins testify against us: for our transgressions are with us; and as for as our iniquities we know them.*" The apostle Paul wrote in Romans 8:6: "*To be carnally minded is death, but to be spiritually minded is life and peace.*"

It really only takes a second, however, to repent and God is right there beside you. If you get in a place where you feel you cannot hear from God, then dig into His Word. Immerse yourself in God. It will help clear your mind to hear Him more effectively.

For more Scriptures on hearing God's voice, please refer to the appendix at the back of this book.

Remember this:

- God leads us through His Word and the more you know His Word, the easier it is to "hear" his voice on the inside.

- God often leads you by the peace in your heart. If you feel uncomfortable on the inside, take time to pray through.

Chapter 15

God Is a Good God

When I consider the goodness of God and His love for His children I am overwhelmed and encouraged. Jesus states in Matthew 5:45 that it rains on the just and the unjust, but there are many more promises and blessings given to the born-again believer than given to the ungodly. *Born again* means "being transferred into God's family through salvation." It can be achieved by just believing in Jesus Christ and asking Him to be the Lord of your life. With salvation comes all the blessings found in the Old Testament and the New Testament, but the greatest blessing is walking in the love of God.

In Luke 12:7 Jesus said the Father God notices when a sparrow falls to the ground and we are worth more than many sparrows. Even the very hairs of our head are numbered. God cares about what happens to us—even the minute details. Jesus told Nicodemus in John 3:16 that God loved the world so much that He gave His only son that whoever would believe on Him would not perish but have everlasting life.

God Wants You to Prosper

The Lord is even interested in our prosperity and our health. There are many times when He tells us these truths but the one I like the best is Third John 1:2: *"Beloved, I pray that you may prosper in all things and be in health, just as your soul prospers"* (NKJV).

John 10:10 tells us Jesus came to give us life and that we might have it more abundantly—not just ordinary life, but abundant life. What a Savior!

Jesus wants us to move ahead from glory to glory—to be successful in our Christian walk and in our relationship with Him (see 2 Cor. 3:18). In Romans 8:29 Paul tells us the work of the Holy Spirit will help us to be like Jesus or to be transformed into His image. Even the Old Testament has so many peeks into the heart of God of His desire to bless His children.

For the eyes of the LORD run to and fro throughout the whole earth, to show Himself strong on behalf of those whose heart is loyal to Him (2 Chronicles 16:9 NKJV).

The Lord Cares for Us

The Psalms are full of God's care and willingness to defend His own. One of my favorites is Psalm 121:8: *"The LORD will guard your going out and your coming in from this time forth and forever"* (Ps. 121:8 NASB).

The Lord Delights in Us

Psalm 37:23 says the steps of a good man are ordered of the Lord and He delights in his way. He delights in us. Verse 4 says if we delight in Him, He will give us the desires of our heart.

One day I was saying to the Lord that I delight in Him and then I told Him what I wanted. I felt He was laughing at me, so I asked Him why He was laughing. He said that He gave me those desires in the first place.

The Lord Has Good Plans for Us

Jeremiah 29:11 says that the Lord has good plans for us and our future. And we can find Him if we search for Him with all our heart (see Jer. 29:13).

I often refer to this if I am feeling down. I remind my-self that God has good things in store for me! This is a promise you should memorize:

> For I know the plans I have for you," declares the LORD, "plans to prosper you and not to harm you, plans to give you hope and a future (Jeremiah 29:11 NIV).

The Lord Forgives and Forgets

In Psalm 103 we see God's forgetfulness also shows His great love for us:

> As far as the east is from the west, so far has He removed our transgressions from us. As a father has compassion on His children, so the LORD has compassion on those who fear Him; for He knows how we are formed, He remembers that we are dust (Psalm 103:12-14 NIV).

He forgives our sins and forgets them if we just ask:

> If we confess our sins, He is faithful and just to forgive us our sins, and cleanse us from all unrighteousness (1 John 1:9).

For more study on the goodness of God, please refer to the appendix at the back of the book.

Changing History

God loves us enough to allow us to change history by praying through. George Washington impacted history by praying when he knelt in the snow at Valley Forge and changed the direction of the Revolutionary War. Hezekiah cried to the Lord in Second Kings 19:14 when Sennacherib was a threat to Israel, and God did miracles to spare them. Later when Hezekiah was dying, he prayed and the Lord gave him 15 more years and even gave him a sign that he was healed by pushing back the sun dial 10 degrees (see 2 Kings 20:10-11). You can change history in your own life and in your own time by praying through. It's a marvelous gift and a wonderful adventure.

God is a good God and He loves us dearly. I hope my life experiences will help you in your walk with Jesus Christ your Savior. Remember, you are under the care of the Great Creator of the universe, God the Father, and you have the constant help of the precious Holy Spirit who wants to dwell in you and keep you in everything you do. When you pray, always listen for His leading on the inside. He will help you to always pray through.

Appendix

Scriptures on the coming of the Holy Spirit:

Acts 9:17, 1 Corinthians 14:18, Acts 11:15-18, Acts 19:1-6, Ephesians 1:13 14, Joel 2:28-29, Isaiah 28:11; 44:3, Zechariah 12:10, Matthew 3:11, Mark 1:8; 16:17, Luke 3:16; 11:13; 24:49, John 1:33; 4:14; 7:37-39; 14:16-26; 15:26; 16:7-14.

Scripture references where Jesus cast out demons:

Mark 9:25, Mark 1:23-28, Luke 4:33-37, Mark 6:7-13, Luke 13:10-17, Matthew 9:32,33, Mark 7:25-30, Matthew 15:22-28, Mark 9:14-29, Matthew 17:14-21, Luke 9:37-42.

Scriptures on hearing God's voice:

Psalm 37:23, Romans 2:4, Matthew 7:7-8, Luke 1:79, Psalm 119:105, James 1, James 3:17, John 10:4, Psalm 116:1,2, Psalm 119:133.

Scriptures on the goodness of God:

Psalm 139, Zechariah 4:10, Psalm 147:11, Proverbs 5:21, Jeremiah 31:33, Psalm 107:20,

John 3:16, Psalm 121:8, Psalm 37:23, Psalm 37:4, Psalm 147:11, 1 Chronicles 16:9, Luke 12:7, Psalm 139:14, Jeremiah 29:11, Psalm 103:12-14, Jeremiah 31:34, Romans 2:4b.

Prayer of Salvation

"Father God, I confess that I am a sinner, but today I believe the Lord Jesus Christ died on the cross for my sins and He was raised from the dead for my justification. I receive and confess Him as my personal Savior."

If you have prayed this prayer, sign your name below and the date. You will always be able to refer to this and remember when you were saved and brought into God's family. It is wonderful to be born again. The Bible tells us that the angels rejoice when someone receives Jesus as their Lord. Your eternal home is now in Heaven and God has great things in store for you here on the earth.

Today _____, I accepted Jesus as my Lord. God is now my Father and my eternal home is in Heaven.

Name: _____

About Sara Steele

Sara Steele is a dedicated follower of Christ with a true heart for prayer. She graduated from Central Bible College in Springfield, Missouri, and was licensed under the Assemblies of God. She and her husband Wilbur served as pastors in Naper, Nebraska; Coleridge, Nebraska; and Yankton, South Dakota. For a number of years Sara served as a state Missionette's director for the Assemblies of God.

Later, Sara discontinued her minister's license and ministered through para-church work. She was president of the local chapter of Women's Aglow and served as a state Women's Aglow Prayer Coordinator as well as a board member of the Women's Aglow Area Board.

Sara has worked in Interfaith Women's Ministry and Women's Prayer and Share for many years. She also has held numerous kids' crusades in various communities.

Sara and Wilbur travel nationwide ministering about prayer and the gifts of the Holy Spirit. They often hold prayer meetings in their home, always welcoming others into the presence of the Lord. They have been married for over sixty years and have four children and eleven grandchildren.

About Susan Janos

Susan Janos has worked in Christian publishing for more than 20 years as a writer, editor, and marketing professional. She is the president of Write Specialists, LLC, a company dedicated to producing excellent written work for the Kingdom of God. For more information visit www.writespecialists.com.

IN THE RIGHT HANDS, THIS BOOK WILL CHANGE LIVES!

Most of the people who need this message will not be looking for this book. To change their lives, you need to put a copy of this book in their hands.

> *But others (seeds) fell into good ground, and brought forth fruit, some a hundred-fold, some sixty-fold, some thirty-fold* (Matthew 13:8).

Our ministry is constantly seeking methods to find the good ground, the people who need this anointed message to change their lives. Will you help us reach these people?

> *Remember this—a farmer who plants only a few seeds will get a small crop. But the one who plants generously will get a generous crop* (2 Corinthians 9:6).

EXTEND THIS MINISTRY BY SOWING
3 BOOKS, 5 BOOKS, 10 BOOKS, OR MORE TODAY,
AND BECOME A LIFE CHANGER!

Thank you,

Don Nori Sr., Publisher
Destiny Image
Since 1982